FOR THE LOVE OF WINE

FOR THE LOVE OF WINE

MY ODYSSEY THROUGH THE WORLD'S MOST ANCIENT WINE CULTURE

ALICE FEIRING

POTOMAC BOOKS

An imprint of the University of Nebraska Press

Library of Congress
Cataloging-in-Publication Data
Feiring, Alice, author.
For the love of wine: my odyssey through the
world's most ancient wine culture / Alice Feiring.
pages   cm
ISBN 978-1-61234-764-6 (cloth: alk. paper)
ISBN 978-1-61234-838-4 (epub)
ISBN 978-1-61234-839-1 (mobi)
ISBN 978-1-61234-840-7 (pdf)
1. Wine and wine making—Georgia
(Republic)—History. 2. Georgia
(Republic)—Description and travel.
I. Title.
TP559.G2F45 2016
338.4'76632094758—dc23
2015034732

Set in Garamond Premier Pro by L. Auten.
Designed by N. Putens.

For my brother, Dr. Andrew Jonathan Feiring

*That's why drinking wine is so important in my films.
It brings people together, helps them to discover
something new — maybe even happiness.*

— OTAR IOSSELIANI

CONTENTS

ILLUSTRATIONS

INTRODUCTION

When I told people that I was traveling to Georgia for wine, invariably the response was, "Great!" Then came the look of confusion as they did a double take and asked, "Umm, how far from Atlanta are the vines?"

"The country of," I'd say, then further clarify that this Georgia was not in the United States. "It's the one under the Caucasus mountain range, not the Blue Ridge."

"Really? They make wines there?"

They sure do, and I adore them.

Georgia is a small and rich country, about the size of West Virginia. On the west is the Black Sea. To the north lies Russia. On the southeast is Azerbaijan and to the south are Armenia and Turkey. Save for Russia (even though it does refer to its vodka as wine) all of those countries have an ancient winemaking heritage; wine origins seem to be in that zone. And they are all clamoring to be called the region of origin of wine. But Georgia might have an advantage. Now sitting in the National Museum in the Georgian capital of Tbilisi is the oldest cultivated grape seed, which carbon dating puts between six and eight thousand years old. But whoever ultimately wins that "We're the oldest" race, Georgia, with its 525 or so indigenous grapes, has the longest unbroken winemaking history. They say it has eight thousand vintages.

What tenacity, despite being battered through centuries by the

Ottomans and the Persian Shah Abbas II, who viciously tore up the grapevines, thinking it was from there that the Georgians derived their strength. They'd been abused under the Russians and then had further suffered the insults of communism. Through it all they never lost their wine tradition. They clung to their *ghvino* (wine) with such a passion you'd think it was their blood. They also clung to a clay pot called a *qvevri*, in which they made their wine with unfailing devotion.

Reading through Henry W. Nevinson's view of Georgia in his 1920 *Peoples of All Nations: Their Life Today and Story of Their Past*, I was struck by how little had changed. Nevinson writes the following about Georgia: "The chief product was wine. The country seems to run with wine. The grapes are squeezed in primitive presses, cleaned with boughs of yew, and the juice run off into huge earthenware vats sunk in the ground, and big enough to hold a man, for when fermentation is finished and the wine drawn off a man gets into the vat to clean it out. The wine is usually poured into tanned buffalo skins, which are laid upon narrow wooden cars and driven slowly along the mountain roads, joggling as they go."

Except for the tanned skins for transport, the process is pretty much exactly as I witnessed in my own travels. What's more, now, as then, the country seems to run with and on wine. According to historian David Turashvili in his book *His Majesty Georgian Wine*, customarily Georgians would first ask about their neighbors' vines and only then ask about their families. Wine is the Georgians' poetry and their folklore, their religion and their daily bread.

What do these ancient yet new wines taste like?

There is red and white wine, of course, but the region is most famous for its white wine, which is actually the amber color of rattlesnake venom. Some call it orange. The color comes from making a white wine as a red wine, with skin contact (see chapter 1). This skin contact not only darkens the color but also lends a sturdy texture. Many of the Georgian wines are tannic, like the tannin in a cup of green tea. On the palate there can be sensual explosions of blossom water and honey without the sweetness; there can be exotic, church-evocative spices of myrrh and frankincense and often a nut of juiciness in the middle.

The reds are far from stereotypical, ranging from large and powerful to delicate and light. Flavors can call to mind the desert or the mountains. But with so many different varieties of grapes and variations of soils, there's a spectrum of tastes.

In a traditional winery one won't find the familiar wooden barrels. Instead the historical and favored vessels for fermentation and storage are the qvevri, the huge earthenware vats sunk in the ground that Nevinson wrote about. They are particular citron-shaped amphoras, made of the local terra-cotta, sealed, sanitized on the inside with propolis, and strengthened with a lime paint or concrete on the outside. They are buried in the ground, where they can survive safely as long as there are no earthquakes, for generations. And now the qvevri have a stamp of approval from the United Nations.

In 2013 the United Nations acknowledged their importance by awarding the qvevri a place on the UNESCO Intangible Cultural Heritage list. Ultimately the award is no more than a bit of applause for the home country and a vote that says, "Hey, world, the qvevri needs to survive." So along with the Argentine tango and traditional violin making in Cremona, as well as the polyphonic songs of Georgia, this, the original container for making wine, is deemed not to be just a museum piece but also a living tradition. Clay — not just in qvevri, but particularly in qvevri — is having its star moment.

The winemaking world is currently crazy for making wine in clay pots, qvevri or otherwise. There is someone making them in Texas. An Italian company named Clayver is producing and marketing a variant on the clay qvevri that it claims is an improvement on a vessel that has been performing beautifully for eight thousand vintages. There are conferences on clay vessels in Tuscany. Winemakers from Australia to South Africa, in France and Italy, are making wine in them. There are tastings in London devoted to them. Other nations have a history of making wine in clay; after all, before there was glass, clay was *the* container, but whether the pot is a *dolia, giara,* or *tinaja,* the Georgian qvevri, with its great-great-grandmother status, is at the top of the heap.

Another reason Georgia has become an unlikely darling is that little has changed in its winemaking technique over the centuries.

With little bowing to fashion, it fits right into today's clamoring for the wines that are called "natural." Organic viticulture: nothing added and nothing taken away.

And so the remote country and its forty or so (and increasing steadily) commercial natural winemakers find themselves the new international heroes in today's wine scene.

However, the new winemakers are at a crossroads. They will be under pressure from chemical and technical companies who want their business and who want to sell them new tools and potions. Some will accuse the wines of having rustic tannins. They will say the taste of Georgia is old-fashioned. They will push them to grow French varietals and install irrigation.

Will the new winemakers have what it takes to battle those marketers who would like them to make more modern wines? Will they be able to resist the technical and chemical companies telling them that they need to make more market-dependable wines? Those are the questions I was asking and the answers I was seeking. Whether I was there at a conference, to consult, to write a project for the government, to attend a book party (mine), or to visit, I wanted to understand if they could succeed in something unparalleled, to resist the pressure to commercialize and homogenize. I hoped they were up to the fight, but I didn't know for sure, though there were clues, embedded deeply within their language and culture.

Perhaps it's a result of Georgia's history of constant invasions that the Georgians have developed a kind of posttraumatic stress disorder that motivates them to defend their vine in a deeper way. This readiness to protect themselves from danger is evidenced in the normal fabric of their society. Take, for example, their common toast, "*Gaumarjos*" — which means "To your victory" — or the variation on hello, "*Gamarjoba*," which has a similar meaning.

The reference to war and victory is the result of historically vicious attacks from groups that have included Assyrians, Arabs, Persians, and Mongols from the east and Greeks, Romans, and (notably) Turks from the west. Before that, the country had survived the religious invaders. The bloodshed was particularly vicious in the east of the country, in the region of Kakheti. After all these attacks the beleaguered country was finally absorbed into the Russian empire, only to endure decades of Soviet industrialization. In an illustration of "destroy what you love," during the seventy years of Soviet domination, the Russians, with their goal of increased production at the cost of quality, not only reduced the country's varieties to only two or four grapes but also brought the wine that they revered — the Georgian — down to the lowest common denominator. Through it all the Georgians persevered. They fought for their vine the way some fight for their religion.

The Georgians' wine is their symbol of their survival. And as soon as I sipped my first Georgian wine, their wines and ways became a symbol for my own survival as well. You see, I write about natural wine. Championing the underdog, helping to make room for the authentic that is being lost in an age of industrialization — this is what I'm known for.

Making wine with the philosophy of nothing added or taken away has been growing exponentially in the past decade. Right now much of the rest of the world is returning to the specific winemaking philosophy Georgia has always held dear. It's nothing short of a revolution. The Georgians have been passionate, religious, and stubborn about it. They had little idea, though, that they had like-minded sisters and brothers in other countries or that they had something to teach the rest of the world about commitment to organic viticulture and minimalist winemaking.

My first visit to the country was in 2011 for the First International Qvevri Symposium. I was struck by the richness of the culture, the music, the food, and the Georgian passion for them all. But I was also impressed by the deliciousness and honesty of the wine. I had never been exposed to a country where wine was so profoundly woven into customs and daily life. The Georgians also showed me they were serious about continuing to work naturally when a group cobbled together the funds to translate my second book, *Naked Wine: Letting Grapes Do What Comes Naturally*, into their language. The government, instead of fighting natural (the way they do in France or Italy), put money behind the wine's promotion. While there's room for both kinds of wines in the world, Georgian government agencies understood that Georgia's continued recognition would not be for the more inexpensive wines from big companies but for the boutique operations, the organic wines made with little intervention, the wines stripped back to show the natural beauty of the people and the place.

Georgia was motivated, and I had a new wine cause. It became important to me to give these traditional and natural wines enough love and attention so that they'd have a secure place on the wine shelves, in the hope that Georgian winemakers wouldn't have to resort to making common wines from common grapes in an international style. They needed to celebrate their individuality. That's where their hearts were. That's what the world needed. I didn't want them to make the same mistakes that other countries that had emerged from Soviet regimes had made: entering the wine market, they had ripped out their indigenous grapes and replaced them with ubiquitous ones, giving up their traditional fermenting vessels for newfangled fads, whether stainless or toasty new oak. Those wines lost their accents. They tried to become like the Chilean or the Californian, and they failed in their mission to gain global recognition. In the end those wines were not true to themselves, their country, or their lineage.

On that first trip to Georgia, I saw that the country was eager for all sorts of opinions and consultants. Winemakers wanted to know how their *ghvino* measured up. During that trip I bumped into a man I knew from California. He was a winemaker. He was a thoughtful man, but he also sold additives and machines, one of which separated wine into sludge, water, and alcohol so that the winemaker could reconstitute it. I was upset to see him in Georgia and worried that his presence there signaled the possibility of his, as well as others', meddling with the Georgians' ancestral wine practices. So I summoned my courage to tell him to keep his tricks away from Georgian wine or I would turn into a strong warrior unafraid to protect what she loved.

FOR THE LOVE OF WINE

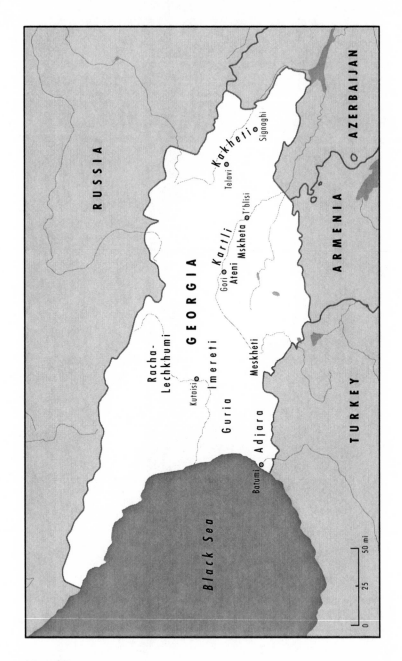

Map of Georgia.

CHAPTER I

JET LAG AND THE CHALLENGE

After another gulp of an amber-hued wine, all I could think of was bed. I'd endured a twenty-hour travel day and was impossibly jet-lagged while life was bursting all around me in the crumbling sandstone Georgian city of Tbilisi. I was with my friend John Wurdeman, a burly expat and owner of the winery Pheasant's Tears, which had made the wine in my glass. John tried to rouse me out of my stupor and pushed the addictive Georgian cheese bread, *khachapuri*, my way.

Sitting in the outdoor café after a heady meal, I was lost in a blur of the country's exotica, blue fenugreek, and marigold flowers—spices that help make the Georgian cuisine justifiably famous. But the natural wine of Georgia, like the one in my glass, was the real reason I was here now and had returned repeatedly to this country. It was spicy, strong, varied stuff. While commercial winemaking is still in its infancy (many producers were just emerging from making wine for their families and bottling commercially for the first time), the potential for further greatness is all there. And it's not just because of Georgia's 525 (and counting) unique grape varieties or even that it has an unbroken tradition of vinifying in the qvevri, which has become the newest fad in the western world. Another gift Georgian winemakers have given to the New World is making wine with what is known in the business as "skin contact." White wine in that country is made like red wine, in contact with the skins. Instead of being pressed off their skins immediately (so that the wines have a gentle straw color, almost clear) the grapes stay with their skins for up to eight months and, on rare occasions, longer. This process has resulted in tastes in wine that are exotic—beeswax and orange blossom water and strawberry tea, in addition to the wine's bitter and savory power; this process was the emotional thread that drew me in. It was the depth of natural Georgian wine culture. Those who made wine naturally with an eye to tradition were at risk. The little guy is always in danger, and championing the little guy has become my life's purpose.

"So let's figure this out. Where do you need to go?" John said.

John was helping me arrange my plans, which as of my arrival were still unformed. "I need to go out west. All I know is this region, Kakheti," I said. That was where John's winery was and where the lion's share of the country's wine production was focused. "So Imereti, Racha, those places for sure. I want to see what once was and what can be. Mostly I just need to get the feel for the land and the people."

He nodded his head.

I can't overstate how remarkable I find it that the Georgian approach to wine production has survived vicious invasions by those who have banished and pulled out native vines, and that it has survived the assault from Soviet industrialization. But could it survive the influence and seduction of the international wine market? Could Georgians resist the onslaught of wine consultants intent on modernizing their tradition? Could they resist chemical salesmen trying to infiltrate both the wineries and the vineyards? Many emerging countries have lost their identities and traditions once they have entered competitive foreign markets. Take, for example, Greek wines. Back before, let's say 2002, the vines were all Athiri, Roditis, and Mavrodaphne. Then came an influx of European money, and there was a rush to modernize, to buy new oak barrels and technology, and the Cabernet and Merlot vines were sunk into the ground. The new Greek wines tasted placeless. Most of them still do, though that is finally beginning to swing around. A few years back Bulgaria made a big pitch to American wine writers. In a test tasting in a marketing office its winemakers showed off their

Syrah and their Chardonnay. We writers told them the world doesn't need another oaked Chardonnay; what it needs is a true Bulgarian experience. I've yet to have a wine made from Mavrud, but Bulgarian Cabernet? Even though I don't need it to enrich my life, I admit I've tasted it.

Georgia almost made this misstep. I saw this soon after I had my first Georgian wine in 2008.

It was a Kisi.

I was thrilled by it, and when in 2009 Georgia came to New York to show its wines, I was first to arrive. I was dismayed. Instead of the wines made in ancient pots from rare grapes, the only wine made in qvevri came from a winery named Pheasant's Tears. What's more, there were almost more Chardonnays and Merlots than I could find in Napa. I left thinking it was just another sad story of a country coming onto the international market. But just a few years later, in 2011, when I visited Georgia for the first time, I realized that there was another spirit that was indomitable, and that was the one I cared about. I hoped that Georgian winemakers could do what few before them had been able to do: stay true to themselves. I sensed there was enough pride in the Georgian character to safeguard traditions and to not fall for the quick money trick of entering the market with a cheapened product. Yes, I sensed it, but was it true? For my own satisfaction, I wanted to explore. I wanted to go deep into the people, to travel, to drink, and to debate. I wanted to find out if there was enough common sense, enough pride in Georgia's history, to resist the pratfalls of modern winemaking marketing pressure. But not that night.

As if sensing my yearning to go to bed, another of the natural wine gang, Niki Antadze, showed up to transport me to his parents' house, where I was crashing. Wearing dark glasses and sporting a not quite freshly shaved chin, he looked like a perfect French film noir star. Actually Niki — son, father, husband, former ski instructor, club owner, and royal before the Soviet invasion — is a serious winemaker. I had met John and Niki on that first visit to Georgia in 2011 and have seen them since in different countries — more often, in fact, than I see my friends who live uptown in New York.

Niki eased into our booth. John poured him a glass of the Kisi we were drinking and the two of them talked about their plans for me. Usually I liked to go it alone. A car and a playlist was all that I needed. But on this trip it was finally time for me to try to understand where Georgia had come from and where it was going, so I'd be handed off from one winemaker to the next, like some game of Pass or Perish football.

Niki took off his Ray-Bans, lit up a Marlboro, and started talking to John in rhythmic Georgian, a language in which — after about four words — I was lost. "Don't worry," said John, seeing my wrinkled brow. "It's going to be great."

When Niki finally said to me, "Let's go," I quickly raised my glass, exclaimed "Gaumarjos!" and flamboyantly drained it Georgian style. I gave John a kiss on the cheek, and we walked toward Niki's car on Leselidze Street.

In the car he said, "It is good to see you."

It was always good to see Niki and be around his energy, which sometimes was so zen that I thought of him as the Skinny Buddha.

"How is your brother?" he asked.

My brother was in trouble. "The chemo stopped working. He had been going into the hospital a couple of days a week, but he can't anymore. He has hung up his stethoscope. He's feeling useless and irrelevant."

He shook his head. What else could he say, although the feeling of compassion was there. He started up the car. He had a detour in mind. "Friends of mine are having a party."

Niki always knew where the parties were.

"You know that cooking school I told you about, Culinarium?"

So much for bed.

After a few hairpin turns, passing the late-night vegetable stalls that never seem to close, we got out of the car in the artsy Vera neighborhood. We walked past the darkened square, where people were laughing, smoking, joyously just being. We reached an unmarked door, and Niki pushed it open. Inside was a gleaming stainless test kitchen stacked with the city's smartest, coolest, most cosmopolitan professionals, all toting cocktails. I immediately felt frumpy, unshowered, gritty from the plane, shorter, and a good twenty years older than everyone else. I sampled whatever was in everyone's martini glasses, but it was sweet — strange for a country where bitter and compelling are more common than sweet.

"This is my friend Alice," Niki explained to a man who I understood was a business partner of Tekuna Gachichiladze, the chef who ran the school. He was pleasant looking, if a little guarded. "She's a wine writer from New York City."

Seeing that I was taken care of, Niki deserted me for his friends.

"A wine writer? And you're here for Georgian wine?" he asked me.

"Of course," I answered.

"What have you done since arriving?" he asked.

Trying to sip the too-sweet cocktail, I responded, "I ate a radish that burst with such juiciness it was shocking."

For some reason he was unimpressed. I tried again. "Then I fell in love with sour, bitter, yogurt soup. It's hard to find in the States."

I was suddenly self-conscious about my passion for food and flavor, and I feared he must have thought I was a freak.

"Would you like a glass of wine?" he asked, noticing my barely touched drink.

The wine he was offering me was from a box in the corner, which was labeled "Provençe rosé." This is exactly the kind of wine I avoid: processed, mass-produced, and highly sulfured. But in Georgia you accept hospitality even if it consists of a wine you'd rather not smell, let alone drink. You must, or you risk insulting your host. I said, "Of course."

He twisted the spout, and I could tell by the smell that it was going to taste like a long-lost, shriveled cucumber from the bowels of a neglected refrigerator. He tried to reassure me: "It's cheap and it's good."

It might have been cheap, but it was anything but good. I set the glass down while he settled on the adjacent stool.

He then bragged that he was planning to study for a prestigious certification in London that could lead to the ultimate credential in wine education, Master of Wine. "I'm taking the WSET exam."

"Really," I said. I was trying to comprehend how he was planning to study wine yet didn't have the awareness to know he was pouring me crap.

"'I'm going to be leading more wine classes here, so I wanted some credentials. Bio wine is bullshit," he said. "It doesn't make a difference in the taste, and it's too expensive."

Reaching for a glass of water, I pondered how a thinking person could actually believe agriculture was irrelevant to flavor. It was confounding, but I saw it frequently: people who were committed to organic produce forgot that grapes that made wine were produce as well. This wasn't a Georgian problem alone; it was global. It was commonplace to eat organic yet drink conventional. It is a disconnect that makes no sense to me. So I said to him, "But your cooking school is about quality ingredients. Why wouldn't you do the same with wine?"

"It's all the same."

"You are taking wine classes to be an expert, and you think all wine, conventional or natural, is the same?"

"Well, of course it's not. There are different grapes; there are good wines and bad wines."

"But you like organic food, don't you? Most of the food made in Georgia is grown organically."

"Food here is cheap. Wine should be too," he argued.

I certainly agreed that wine should be affordable, but I know I overpay at the Greenmarket to support my farmers so that they stay in business. And I am willing to do that—as long as it's not crazy—for wine.

I pushed back. I pointed out that he was suffering from the same affliction as many of the food-obsessed around the globe: lower standards for wine than for food. Gaining momentum, I said, "So you go to the foreign-owned Carrefour and pick up some dreck French wine instead of supporting homegrown artisans? I understand the need for inexpensive party wine, but it reflects on your taste, on your philosophy, no? Is your cooking school cheap?" The Georgian wine-and-food-pairing class he was offering later in the week was going to cost $125. I continued: "But Niki makes organic wine. Do you like his?"

"Niki's wines, well, they're special." He seemed to use "special" in the way the French do: as a synonym for "eccentric" or "peculiar."

One has to be special to make wine the way Niki does. He, like those of his generation, as well as the generations before him, had always longed to make wine. But it was not an approved profession in Soviet times. Unless one worked for a state wine factory, the only legal way to make wine was for personal consumption. Most who lived in the countryside had their little *marani* (winery) with some buried qvevri. A decade after perestroika, dreams of something more started to take hold among those who had wine production in their veins. Niki had felt a growing desire to go back to his roots. "My grandmother told me that the family made wines in Manavi. She showed me a plot of land and proclaimed, 'That's the spot for Mtsvane,'" he'd once told me. In 2006 he bought three hectares where his ancestors had once worked the land, left the club and ski life, and gambled his family's future on the hope that he could grow vines organically and make wine in qvevri. Of course he was "special." What kind of person has the patience to wait until 2013 to release his 2008 Mtsvane because it was only ready to drink then?

Here Niki's friend was blasé about it all; he didn't appreciate the difference in the tastes of his local wines. He wanted them to lose their individuality; he wanted them to be unrecognizable from, let's say, those of Chile. He thought it weird that the traditional whites of Georgia were made as if they were reds, with extended skin contact. This skin contact, rare for white wines, is what gives them strength, backbone, tannin, and color—giving them the name "orange wines"—and stability. And yes, the cooking school business partner was correct: they weren't cheap. But for the most part they weren't ridiculously expensive either. Given their quality, the fact that most are available under twenty-five dollars a bottle is extraordinary. Given the love, care, and work put into every bottle, they are far less expensive than, say, Italian wines made in this fashion.

The thought that this man was about to get a useless degree in order to pose as an expert was utterly depressing to me. His attitude about wine was the danger that the new and hopeful cohort of natural winemakers in Georgia were up against. I had seen the same thing in New York; I had seen it in Paris and Rome. But I was sad to see it in Tbilisi, in a country with such a long-standing tradition of natural wine and winemaking.

It wasn't too much later that Niki finally nodded to me that we could go. It was early in the morning, and the city people were still enjoying the nearby park and a photography installation that was flashing between the trees in the dark. I was upset, but Niki, ever composed and rational, wasn't. "He's a good man," he said. "When fashion changes, he'll change as well." Then he told me of his own plans. He was starting to complete his winery. It was to be near his vines in Manavi. He would build a little hut to sleep near the vines; the walls of his winery would be fabricated by laying in straw bales. He would have about three months to finish the work, yet he hadn't broken ground.

"You're really going to have it in time for this year's vintage?" I asked, incredulous, forgetting that even though the country is notoriously on GMT—Georgian Maybe Time—when there's motion, things can happen quickly.

He shrugged as if to say, "If God wills it."

His car climbed the hills outside of the city to the quiet place where his parents' house was located, where I could finally fall into bed. As I lay there, I berated myself for not being harder on his cooking school friend. But as I fell asleep, I thought to myself: there are some people I can take on in person; others I take on in print.

MATSONI SOUP

This hot soup is so soothing after one has stepped off a plane at the end of a red-eye; there's something healing about its complex tang. Most of the world's yogurt soups rely on garlic for flavor, but in Georgia it is the high acid yogurt they call *matsoni* and the fresh herbs that really deliver the punch. What's more, it's an essential food to have in one's quiver when traveling in a country of hard drinkers, as it's the traditional hangover remedy.

On one of my first nights in Georgia, I convinced Niki's mother to share her recipe with me. But it was on later visits that I had a lesson in making the soup from John Wurdeman's friend Lia, who went into more detail about the soup-making technique. There are many variations, and from what I could see, as is usual, every family has its own particular twist. Some recipes call for the inclusion of rice. I prefer it without.

Here I've blended my favorite elements from Lia's and Niki's mom's recipes. For example, in Kakheti, where Lia is from, they'd never use tarragon, but in Tbilisi? Sure. And I loved it. For best results, make your own yogurt from raw milk.

A hangover isn't a prerequisite for enjoyment.

2 cups *matsoni* (yogurt)
2 cups water (if using Greek yogurt, use twice the amount of water)
1 tablespoon wheat flour
1 onion, finely chopped
½ stick of butter
1 egg, beaten
2 sprigs coriander, dill, or tarragon
freshly ground pepper

Beat yogurt, water, and wheat flour together.

Stew the finely chopped onion in the butter in a saucepan. Pour the beaten yogurt over the onion and boil for 15 minutes, stirring frequently with a spoon.

While slowly stirring the onion and yogurt mixture, pour in the beaten egg. Keep the mixture heated without bringing it to the boiling point. Then remove the saucepan from the fire.

Immediately add shredded coriander, dill, or tarragon.

Add salt to taste.

CHAPTER 2

OF PROPHETS
AND TOASTING

In 2011, before my first visit to Georgia, the wine director for the fancy restaurant Le Bernardin sat in my living room for the purpose of tasting some qvevri wines. I poured the Pheasant's Tears 2009 Rkatsiteli, which I thought lovely. He was amused, but was he smitten? No. In all fairness his clientele were the posh. Without a doubt that amber-colored wine with some tannic scratch would be too shocking for the Manolo Blahnik set. But more used to wines made naturally, I was thrilled by them. Feeling almost bored by the wines around me, these seemed fresh.

Tasting the qvevri wines that first time was the beginning of infatuation for me, and it was with a quick yes that I agreed to travel to Georgia to give a talk on natural wines at the First International Qvevri Symposium in 2011. I traveled like crazy; I had long ago stopped counting the stamps in my passport, but I hadn't experienced this sense of adventure on this level for a long time.

When explaining my next trip to my brother on the phone, I said, "The conference is hosted by the Georgian Orthodox Alaverdi Monastery, a sixth-century church, and a cleric named Bishop Davit—a wine loving ex–cave dweller—and it's funded in part by USAID."

"It sounds like that Sacha Baron Cohen movie, *Borat*, doesn't it?" he laughed. "This is really funny."

But it soon got serious, even though entering the former Republic of Georgia was like stepping through the wardrobe. Most international flights land and leave at three in the morning. I felt the astonishing, surreal whoosh as we lowered to the ground into the land of saturated colors and flavors. How could I not connect to a place that counted a medieval epic poem about friendship, sex, and unconditional love as one of its national treasures? I had prepared for the trip by reading it: *The Knight in the Panther's Skin* by Shota Rustaveli. This is the story of how two accidental friends for life risk limb and soul to find a woman who has stolen one of their hearts. Like much of Georgian history, it is ancient. The emotional memory, however, is fresh.

After traveling for so long, I collapsed in exhaustion an hour before dawn in a lopsided bed in a tiny hotel just outside the old city of Tbilisi. The crumble of its stone reminded me of Fez but without the calls to Allah and without the donkeys. A few hours after landing, I groggily emerged into the brilliant sunlight and took in the landscape dominated by a fifty-foot statue. It was a 1950s Soviet-era rendition of Mother Georgia. One of her hands was on a sword, and the other held a *piala*, the terra-cotta wine cup. She loomed over the other super-modern structures, like the steel and glass worm-like bridge crossing the Kura River.

On the way to lunch at a local bean restaurant, I savored the cheesy bread, *khachapuri*. I had my first glimpses of the flavors and colors. I felt an affinity with it all. Why? In part because I so often feel too emotional to live in the real world, but in Georgia everyone seemed like a mythical human who felt first and thought later. I felt at home. Perhaps my grandfather was from Georgia instead of being a White Russian from across the Black Sea because the faces, the food, and the colors all seemed so familiar. The dumplings the Georgians call *kinkhali* were like my grandmother's pillowy *kreplach*. The beans reminded me of a vegetarian cholent. The pickles on the table reminded me of any meal of my childhood home. Then the way everyone spoke with such excitability made me feel that everything about Georgia was like a blood tie. Whether or not there was a genetic or spiritual link, Georgia, in the shadows of the Caucasus Mountains, burrowed under my skin.

It was in Tbilisi that I met John H. Wurdeman V, one of the event's organizers and the co-owner of Pheasant's Tears winery. I found him to have an uncanny likeness to Russell Crowe, with a heavy straight blond ponytail and sky blue eyes. I was already acting on instinct, and I skipped the bus to the conference and claimed my seat as passenger in his car and claimed John as my friend, only to find a copy of my book, *Naked Wine*, in his glove compartment. Yes, I was flattered.

Not only was he an adept translator, but he was also a natural raconteur. Over the course of the next few days, stories bled out of him. The one about how an expatriate, a peasant, and a bishop banded together to bring life back into a wine culture ready to breathe its last breath grabbed me the most. His own story was practically made for the movies, and it went mostly as follows.

John, originally from Virginia, a vegetarian-from-birth son of hippies, was also a talented painter who had studied art in Moscow. After graduation, in search of the multilayered folk music of Georgia, he hitchhiked with his easel; working his way through the flatlands, he reached the hilltop town of Signaghi.

The year was 1996, a time when Georgia was post-perestroika and just settling down from the civil wars that had bloodied the country. The hope for plumbing and peace was beginning. As the sun had long set, traveling John needed a place to sleep. There was one choice in the town.

"I walked in. The electricity was out—lights were always going out back then," John told me. "I asked the man at the desk for a room. There was one regular priced and one deluxe for just a few pennies more. I took the deluxe. But when I got up there, there was no water or heat, of course, because of the electricity outage. I went back down and asked what the differences in the rooms were. Blowing smoke in my face, as if it was perfectly obvious, he said, "One has a view and one doesn't."

"In the morning I looked out the window. Fog sat on the hills below, the clay rooftops of the village peeked out from it. The air was still. The landscape was majestic. The sun was trying to shine on the Caucasus. How could anything be so beautiful?"

Always decisive, he vowed to move there. Just like that. Not only did he fall for the location, but in time he also fell for a town girl, Ketevan, a folk dancer and singer. However, she wouldn't marry him until she had the blessing of her spiritual father, the aforementioned Bishop Davit. One day, when the cherry blossoms burst, she took him to see her bishop, a man with a wild beard and sensitive, all-knowing eyes.

The verdict was a happy one but came with a caveat. If John agreed to see the bishop once a month to talk about art and spirituality, then yes, the couple could marry and start a family. Eventually they would also talk about wine and the bishop's plans to rehabilitate the old winery at Alaverdi.

One child was born and then another. John and his wife traveled the regions collecting songs, tunes, and folk traditions. He painted. They didn't have money, but life was rich.

One day, while John was in the field at work, a brush in hand, a farmer on a noisy tractor drove up to him. The man was devoid of artifice, and after the *gamarjoba*, the obligatory greeting, he skipped the small talk. "I know about everything you're doing for folk traditions," the man on the tractor said. "Wine is no less important. You and I? We need to talk."

The tractor was so cacophonous that John yelled back, "How can we talk when I can barely hear you over that engine? Can't you turn it off?"

The man shouted back, "My starter is busted. Listen, my name is Gela Patashvili from the village of Bodbis Khevi. Everyone knows me. Come to dinner tonight and we'll talk." Gela drove away.

But John, having never agreed, stayed home that night with his family.

Not long after, there was a knock at John's door at dusk. Harvest was under way, and John was surprised to see Gela, fresh from crushing grapes. John invited him in for a bite, for a glass of spirit, but Gela stayed at the door. "You have children; bring them to harvest and then stomp the grapes and see the magic, and then you will reconsider."

John said he would bring them by. But he didn't.

The end of harvest was near. Once again at the end of a long day there was a knock at John's door. Once again, it was Gela. "You don't come to the grapes; I bring the grapes to you. And then we'll talk."

Gela had ferried with him in the back of his truck a quarter of a ton of grapes as a present for John. The artist had no choice but to gather his family and stomp them up. The juice was poured into glass jars to ferment and bubble away as there was no access to a qvevri. But John knew when he was beaten. He agreed to have dinner with the determined farmer and hear more about what he had to say. He was convinced that at most he'd come away with a new friend; a life in wine was certainly not for him.

John and Gela sat outside in the night, and Gela's mother prepared a convincing meal. They drank wine. They drank the local brandy, called *chacha*, the eau-de-vie or grappa-like elixir Ketevan declares is the direct path to heaven. Gela pled his case. He said they'd been making wine in his family as far as he could trace back — some eight generations. Then Gela told him, "Georgia has 520 grape varietals that grow nowhere else in the world. We've survived invasions. We survived when marauders yanked out our vines and burned them. We survived the phyloxera, the louse that eats the vines, by replanting. Then the Soviets reduced our grape varieties to those that were easiest to grow, forgetting the others. They moved the vines from the hills to the flats. If that wasn't bad enough, there are people wanting to imitate international style, Bordeaux-like wines. Merlot and Cabernet! In my country! They are making wine in small barrels, not in the qvevri. This is wrong. Our value is in keeping the character of our wines true to their origins. We have much to offer the world, and if someone doesn't start focusing on our traditional methods, we risk being lost."

John had other priorities, like art, music, and making a living. He was smart enough to know that winemaking wasn't the best way to ensure his family's security. And he wasn't a farmer. He told Gela he would think about it but did not. Gela was undeterred.

In the next conversation they had, he appealed to John's second weakness after art: music. "You collect songs — if they don't get recorded and taught they will die out with the older people. It is the same with the vine. The last people who know the old remedies for taking care of them without chemicals are dying. We need to preserve the knowledge so it can continue. I can do it. I know I can do it. But I need some investment. I need help to buy some land." Then he added, "I need you."

John was not all that seduced by the winemaking experience—he loved to drink, but he had his art on his brain. However, John had a spiritual bent. He didn't have to be swallowed up by a big fish like Jonah to take a hint. He recognized destiny when he saw it. He knew how essential wine was to feastings and gatherings, but it wasn't until that moment that he understood it as an essential thread in the fabric of the country and the people. The painter pulled together some funds, and his small vineyard was started. In the end, the Pheasant's Tears wine project took off and, with eleven organic hectares, became a much bigger part of John's life than he had ever thought it would or should. "As if I didn't have a hard enough time being an artist, now I have two professions that are difficult to make money at," he joked to me.

"When was that?" I asked as we sat in a traffic jam of sheep, which were blocking the road as we headed to his wine bar in Signaghi. This was one of the reasons a thirty-mile trip could take two hours.

"Vintage 2007," he said.

"And why did you decide to work with qvevri? Back then many people were using oak."

Working on the cheap, he and Gela went to an abandoned winery and found some intact qvevri to dig up and replant, allowing them to officially launch their winery with the 2007 vintage. "In 2009 I took the wines—we were only making reds then—to the fair in Prowein in Germany. The feedback I got was that a wine like that could be made only in wood barrels if I was to be taken seriously. I didn't know what to do. I didn't have the money for them. At the time, new oak barrels were $1,000 each. It was the bishop who set me straight."

"Really?" I asked as we started to move on the road, as if wading through the animals.

"He told me that putting a qvevri wine in wood was like putting a bow tie on a Georgian warrior. The bishop was firm on that: "Stay with tradition. Keep true to the Georgian way. Do not improve on what has been tested. Use no additives. Use qvevri. Have faith." In fact he placed his two hands on me at once, saying, "I bless you for never using oak on a qvevri wine."

He gave John the confidence to follow his instinct.

On our last day the symposium group was having lunch in a Kakhetian winery when another group joined us. These were wine professionals brought over by USAID —wine masters, wine educators, and one man in particular that raised a fury in me. At the time he had just sold off his company, Vinovation, to his brother, but he was still connected to it. This company sold reverse osmosis machines, among other technologies. A reverse osmosis machine is something I'd always called a torture chamber for wine. Nothing more than a high-powered filter, it could separate the water and alcohol out of wine so that winemakers could reconstitute the end product to their specifications. Such a procedure is the antithesis of natural winemaking, and I was terrified. I saw this man convincing peasants and government officials that this was the path to success, and if they believed him, honest wine in Georgia would be lost. So I lost all sense of humor and went over to him.

"Hello, Mr. Reverse Osmosis; what do you think of the wines?"

"They need some help," he said.

"Not yours. I just want you to know that if I see you peddling your machines to Georgia, you'll have to contend with me."

I left the country knowing I would return but not foreseeing how often.

Over the next months John decided to instigate getting my book, *Naked Wine*, published in Georgian. I developed a plan and made sure that Gela and John were invited to France for the debut of their wines at the Burning Man of the natural wine world, La Dive Bouteille. I wanted their wines to go to the right people, and the right people would be at that tasting, held yearly on the first weekend in February in the Loire Valley.

That winter I rendezvoused with John and Gela in Paris. We had some walks, a few meals. Gela's first time in France had to be far less colorful than my first time in his country, and he was far less charmed. In fact he was dismayed by the weak wines and the small portions, as well as the meat, which tended to be quite bloody. ("I'm a man, not a wolf," he told John when we were at a wine bar in the Nineteenth Arrondissement.) After a day he was out of patience with concrete; he wanted vines. We started our drive out to the Loire. The first stop was in the little village of Les Montils, just at the beginning of chateau country, at the winery of Thierry Puzelat. Les Montils once had been thriving; now there was just one lonely domaine, that of the Puzelat brothers, rock stars of natural winemaking. Thierry, nearly fifty with impish, high-school-tow-haired-boy good looks, is a good solid drinker, one who likes to fistfight so much that he seems to always sport a good-natured blackened eye and even chuckles about it. I was matchmaking, and I was pleased with myself. After a visit to the vines we ate lunch at Thierry's wife's L'Herbe Rouge Inn. Gela was adventurous and ordered the *boudin noir*. I felt for him as he picked mournfully at the bloody snake of sausage on his plate. But Thierry didn't notice. "So, do you have your wine with you here?"

John did, in fact. He returned from his car with the Pheasant's Tears wines, as well as those of Georgian friends. When the wines had been tasted, I could see Thierry had immediately grasped the situation without needing an explanation about the amber colors, the exotic waxiness, or the absolute life of the wine. It was clear: he was one of them; they were comrades in making wine naturally. He said, "How much do you have? I'll take everything!"

John was confused; was Thierry buying all that wine just for himself? The man was a big drinker, but still that was a lot of wine.

I hadn't yet disclosed to the visitors that Thierry not only made highly regarded wine, but also imported it. Thierry further clarified, "At the Dive, when people ask you who imports your wine to France, you tell them it's me."

At the caves where the Dive was held, Thierry was also showing his own wines, and he was hyping up the Georgians as if they were the new debutantes. That was the beginning of the export expansion of many of the newer Georgian wines as the importers from several countries made their orders. It was a transformational moment for the Georgian wine industry.

During the trip back to Paris, with the glow of that success and with John in the front seat translating, Gela turned his intensity on me. He was insistent on getting my life straight. What I needed was a Georgian husband, to ensure I moved myself to his country. "Good luck with that one," I said. I had recently decided to embrace my singledom and marry the bottle and the vineyard instead of a man. Not that there weren't those who had come around, not that I hadn't loved deeply, but at that point men my age seemed too old and men that were younger were way too young. Then he decided I should stop the life of the struggling writer; what I needed—even if I was going to stay living like a refugee in my New York City Lower East Side walk-up with a tub in the kitchen—was to open a wine bar stocking all of my friends' wines. We drove onward to Paris as Gela continued fixing me and the world. We had no common language, but we knew each other in another way; we would defend each other to the end. It was just instinct.

Perhaps Gela forgot about his great plan for me the night I finally got to go to his house in Georgia and saw him as the prince of his own domaine. Up to that moment I had only seen him as John's partner; this was to be the other side. As the night closed in on the pea-sized early summer grapes, Gela, browned and fit from working the vines, came to welcome us to his home, where he was to be in charge at the very table where he had taken hold of John's destiny. With his dark almond eyes, Gela looked more like a Persian royal than a winemaker. Though I was still stuffed from lunch—enjoyed with Gela's uncle in the woods next to the bee boxes of some itinerant honey makers and which included the tasty, brick-like cornmeal pucks called *mchadi*—I couldn't help but look forward to the meal Gela's wife and mother had prepared for us. The long table was set up outside of the house, and there was barely anything laid out on it, but I wasn't fooled; I knew what was coming. It was going to be a very long night.

Georgians rarely eat. They feast. And these festive spreads are called *supra*. With Gela's uncle I understood that this ritual was religion, and religion meant feasting. Elderly and hunched over, he said to me at his very rustic house, "I live for feasting." And feasting costs money. "Perhaps I should have saved, but life without feasting is meaningless," he said.

The Georgians believe their fairy tales, and one of them is how the land was created. God, you see, was divvying up the land to the people of the world, but the Georgians were too busy feasting to show up to get their cut. When they finally showed up, presumably well fed and having had copious amounts of wine and in tremendously good spirits, they explained their situation with such heartfelt innocence and passion that God realized their sincerity and their enthusiasm for the culture of food and wine, so he gave them the piece he was reserving for himself: Georgia. This might be a story, but the commitment they bring to drinking and eating is a force to deal with. It is no less elaborate than a Jewish seder. It's as if the feast is before God.

The *supra* has rules, and wine is its core. It is a custom that when honored guests arrive, the qvevri is broken into. I followed Gela into the winery, where he knelt down and removed the glass plate on top of the mouth of one vessel, removed the clay seal and then the wooden round board, and siphoned off enough Rkatsiteli for a small army. It was needed.

Friends and relatives started to appear. We had grown to about eighteen people and took our seats at the long table under the star-flecked sky; Gela's mother and wife had sent out the first dishes. Tomatoes and cucumbers; bundles of parsley, dill, and tarragon; and *jonjoli* (pickled wild capers that aren't in fact capers but flowers of the bladderwort tree) were on the table, and our host immediately stood up at the other end of it to lead the feast. He was stepping into roles in which I'd never seen him: patriarch of his home and *tamada*, the toastmaster.

That word, "tamada," translates into English poorly. In truth, the role is closer to a rabbi teaching Talmud study than some comedian presiding over a roast. The word might have come from the remote part of the country, Svaneti, where most archaic forms of the Georgian language are kept alive; it was there they used the word *tamta*. A *tamta* was a work leader in the fields who led the work songs. That very same person, a village wise man or elder, would often be the *tamada*—a term that can be translated as the "leader of the table" and an inspiration for all appetites, including the intellectual.

When I pressed John for more information, he got very Talmudic about the word. Since I spent twelve years in an Orthodox Jewish yeshiva, this kind of symbology was all very familiar to me. "Spelled backward," he said, "'tamada' means 'Adam,' who was the first man, but it also means 'of the earth' or 'of the clay.' Clay is also material for the qvevri. There is a hierarchal structure to the feast in which the *tamada* takes charge of introducing various philosophical subjects for discourse. He oversees which toasts will be drunk from which vessels—the horns called *kantsi*, silver ladles, and clay bowls among some possibilities—or drinking *vakhtangur*-style. That's the practice of drinking with interlocking arms. He also will appoint an *alaverdi* toast, which means the toast is passed on to a specific person who is delegated because the *tamada* believes that person has something pertinent to add to the discussion. The *khorumi*, or pagan priest, would use the *tamada* role to expound on various mystical subjects in pre-Christian times, a usage that was eventually absorbed by the Christian tradition."

No wonder that Georgian feasts are often compared to an academy of learning, a tradition said to stem from the monastery of Ikalto. There the abbot would introduce subjects for discourse in the form of a toast that always delivered important life lessons.

No meal is complete without a series of such toasts, like blessings or Talmudic philosophical offerings. After each toast, cups are knocked back. The silver tipped cow or mountain goat horns, *kantsi*, are passed around and emptied into mouths. It is essential.

There is almost a religious adherence to the hierarchy of the toast. An early one starts with an announcement, such as, "I want to drink to Georgia." From drinking for their country the toasts evolve to cover almost every aspect of life including drinking for the children to drinking for nature, for art, for beauty. Early on in the *supra* there is always a toast for those who are no longer here: "For our ancestors, for our loved ones who have passed on, for the people who made us and are no longer drinking with us," John started to interpret for me as Gela made the memorial toast.

That is a solemn moment, meant to acknowledge lost loved ones. It was inevitable that I would think to my own losses, present and future. On my first trip to Georgia I received a message that a mentor of mine had died, and on this trip to Georgia the threatening illness of my brother was ever present. I had much to cogitate on during this time of the meal.

I imagined my older brother beside me. When we visited together, we became children, of one mind, as close as ever. Yet we had very few shared memories as adults; there were no holidays as a family, just those times when he came out east to see me and our mother. I don't know how that happened. It was Gela who had said vines made more sense to him than many people. The vine has a soul. If the plants don't feel loved, they don't give results. "I'm not talking about drinking," Gela would say. "I'm talking about a relationship." My brother is the rational one to my emotional self; I would have loved to see Georgia drape him in its fairy dust.

Like a skilled actor, Gela held his audience. He told a story about a French winemaker who once asked him what he used for fertilizer. At first Gela didn't understand because the idea of using fertilizer was so alien. Then Gela said, "Every inch of my soil is soaked with the blood of my ancestors. What do you use?"

He went on: "Georgia has been assaulted for centuries. Marauders rushed in and pulled out the vines. Our people were killed. My land is filled with the blood of my ancestors. But this is the strength of the Georgian wine, from our blood-soaked earth. This is our terroir. We had amazing ancestors, and we are walking in their footsteps. We know this. We're always looking for a special result. Why? Our ancestors were real people and lived for real reasons."

Gela expounded further: "But a real person looks for reality in life, constant and powerful. If Georgia didn't have something real about it as an intrinsic quality, it wouldn't be alive today. And' Gela, are not the people who have kept the tradition ali normal people. We open our hearts; what we create w and if the wine is popular, it's because of its authenticit

The table that had been nearly empty at the beginning, with nothing more than the required plates of fresh herbs; braids of tarragon, parsley, and onions; and cucumbers and tomatoes, was rapidly piling high with food: fried eggplants wrapped around garlicky walnut paste, dumplings, fish, breads, *chakapulis* (stews), and the pickles I loved so much.

During a *supra*, food is never removed. It is said that the *supra* continues until every inch of a table is covered with plates, often even two layers of them. The toasts continued. John was on constant translating duty. The wine was constantly replenished. I was glad to not be driving later that day.

I asked Gela what he had learned from his trips to France. He, as he always does, came back with a thoughtful answer that I did not expect: "Georgia can compete with the best of European terroirs, but we need to plant at higher altitudes, as people used to do; we need to go higher and plant more on the slopes. There was wisdom in planting where only grapes can survive, where they have to struggle." If grapes had it too easy, the fruit had less character, just like people.

The poet, winemaker, and wine thinker Ilia Chavchavadze extensively wrote in the late 1800s about wine and the naturalness of the Georgian. One of his comments addressed the notion of land: "We know how to choose the place for vineyards, and it would be impossible for us not to know because cultivating vineyards is not a business that we started yesterday since we have had several centuries experience to make a good choice."

Great terroir always has some degraded rock, limestone, basalt, slate, granite, and schist, along with particular climates. Up until that moment, all of the vineyards I'd seen were in Kakheti. But there were higher elevations in Georgia. I began to hunger, not for food but to see the other terroirs about which Gela knew.

I reached for the bread. I reached for the eggplant. The food, like the wine, went deep down into me. The snap of a radish, as juicy as a cherry. I can't truthfully trace my own heritage to Georgia, but there was something about the country that resonated with me. Georgian food has delicacy, as does, for example, the yogurt soup or the rose petal jam. This is a land where flavor has not been bred out. Georgia is a land that bursts with emotion, flavor, and texture, in people, landscape, food, and — so important — wine.

....

FRIED EGGPLANT WITH WALNUT SAUCE

Walnuts are a key ingredient in Georgian cuisine; they're in sauces, dips, stuffings, and dressings or are just for plain eating. The most typical recipes are vegetables stuffed with a walnut mixture in either a sauce or a paste. Take care; the walnut in Georgia is tender. The closest equivalent I've found in the States are foraged hickory nuts. Those have the desired caramel-like note.

I encountered one of my favorite renditions of this recipe at Gela's the night of the feast. It was simply more fresh and less garlicky than most other examples I'd had, and this is a country not shy of garlic. As with many recipes in Georgia, the preparation relies on a complex mix of spices, including some hard to find outside of Georgia, such as marigold flowers and blue fenugreek. Marigold, often called poor man's saffron, is one of the lesser known of the edible flowers. It adds a dusty assertiveness to the dish and a subtle but perceptible depth. Blue fenugreek (*Trigonella caerulea*; called *utskho suneli* in Georgian, the term translates into the poetic "strange and fragrant smell from far away") seems to have a symbiotic relationship with marigold flowers; the two are often added in equal parts into the recipe.

As far as wine pairings, who cares? Rarely is wine paired with food in Georgia. You just drink through the meal. There's so much variety on the table at any given time that it's ridiculous to try to be classic about it. But if I had to make a stab at it, something with skin contact, Rkatsiteli or Kisi.

Here's a version based on what I had there. Pomegranate seeds are often used for garnish.

1 cup toasted walnuts
⅓ cup packed cilantro leaves

¼ cup packed basil leaves
¼ cup packed parsley leaves
1 teaspoon ground blue fenugreek
1 teaspoon marigold flowers
1 teaspoon wild oregano or wild thyme
½ teaspoon hot paprika
1 tablespoon red wine vinegar
1 clove garlic, minced
½ small yellow onion, roughly chopped
kosher salt and freshly ground black pepper to taste
1½ cups canola oil
4 small Japanese eggplants, trimmed and sliced lengthwise,
     ½ inch thick
½ small red onion, thinly sliced crosswise into rings
pomegranate seeds for decoration and extra pizazz

Place walnuts; half each of the cilantro, basil, and parsley; fenugreek; marigold flowers; oregano or thyme; paprika; vinegar; garlic; yellow onion; salt; pepper; and ⅓ cup water in a food processor; purée until very smooth, about 2 minutes. Take care; you want this to be creamy yet firm, perhaps not soupier than tahini. Set sauce aside.

Heat oil in a 12-inch skillet over medium-high heat. Working in batches, fry eggplant, flipping once, until golden and cooked through, about 4 minutes. Transfer to paper towels to drain and cool; season with salt and pepper.

Spread each slice of eggplant with about 2 tablespoons of the walnut sauce and fold in half; transfer to a serving platter and garnish with remaining cilantro, basil, and parsley leaves and the sliced red onions.

CHAPTER 3

THE LOST ART
OF QVEVRI

"My nickname is Kvevri," Giorgi Barishivilli announced as he opened the gate to his home. This fanatic, who prefers the usage of the older "k" instead of the newer adaptation of "q" for the vessel, was a darkly bearded teddy-bear type. He lived in the long lost capital of Georgia, Mtskheta, twelve miles north of Tbilisi. It is considered holy, a birthplace of Christianity, and a spiritual nerve for Georgia, and tourists are in constant flow to it. Inside the pedestrian streets, peddlers pushed religious relics, crafts, and *churchkela*, the ever-present sausage-shaped dried fruit treat. And there, inside that museum-like village, was the man with a self-proclaimed obsession with qvevri.

Giorgi led me down the few steps to his cellar-sanctuary. It was a three-hundred-year-old rabbit warren filled with his wine and spirit experiments as well as hundreds of antique clay drinking and pouring vessels. They were as orderly as befitted an archivist. Ducking down to avoid head banging on the low ceiling, we entered a room, a study, an ancient man cave lined with vintage photographs; it was where he put down his thoughts and observations with a quill pen loaded with Saperavi ink. We squatted down onto little three-legged stools and were welcomed by firm salty cheese, bread, and fresh walnuts. I asked him what made the best wines.

"The clay must be free of impurities and have the right mix of minerals. It must be porous but not too porous. Where the clay comes from makes a very big difference."

It is the same with wood. Where the oak comes from has a big impact on the flavor from the barrel.

"Some say that the black *qvevri* from the west of Georgia were best," he said.

"Black?" I asked. After all, most of the qvevri I had seen were made of red terra-cotta.

"They came from the west. The clay was mixed with sand and decomposed slate from the Rioni River."

"Why do you say "were," as in the past tense?"

"There are no more qvevri makers there. All dead. No one left to carry on the tradition," he said. "But if you go out to Racha, you might still see some in the ground."

I was soon to go to Racha and would see the Rioni, the river that started in Racha, courses through Kutaisi in Imereti, and ends in the Black Sea. The idea of a pot from the very earth that nurtures wine suddenly seemed like the most perfect container ever in which to express terroir: a wine from slate made in slate. It didn't get any better than that.

As Giorgi talked, I came to see him as another kind of Georgian prophet, one who lived in a little forest hut, whom one went to visit for the wisdom of the ancients. This notion was reinforced when he told me about the mystique of qvevri. "Scientists found heavy metals from chemical farming in the grapes. But after being raised in the vessel, they disappeared. When the wine is made in glass, the metals remain. So, you tell me why. Does the qvevri suck out the metals? We checked them, and no heavy metals were inside the pots. Where did they go?" he said laughing. "We're scratching our heads! But we do know that the wine always reacts to the environment. What we don't know sometimes is why."

"In ancient times, people were buried inside of qvevri-like tombs—like the pyramids. That was the end of life, but the qvevri is the beginning of life for wine," he continued. "It is the womb."

Giorgi told me more of the qvevri's properties. You can keep water in one, above the ground, for a year, but wine, only a month. However, once in the ground, wine keeps indefinitely. "I drank a wine kept in the qvevri for fourteen years, and it was still drinkable. You have to understand that at one time wine was a seasonal beverage. You would drink it until it turned into vinegar. I believe it was the Georgian culture," he said, "that was the first to make wine for multiple seasons."

So it was the qvevri that first made wines safe for the seasons. It was an extraordinary fact to consider. The qvevri must have seemed like a magic pot that could preserve the wine through the dangerous summer months, when wine without preservatives or temperature control could easily be destroyed. Buried in the soil, the qvevri remained cool, keeping the wine stable and safe. The Romans and the Greeks masked the taste of spoiled wine with resins and additives, but in Georgia there was no need to disguise the taste; the wine was built to last. If true, Georgia truly was the beginning of wine civilization.

Giorgi, who, as well as the rest of Georgia, was committed to making wine this way, surely wondered what had taken the rest of the world so long to find them.

Mea culpa.

Clay was the original wine vessel. In the first century BC wood was introduced into the world, and over the centuries it gradually gained ground until, centuries later, clay was forgotten, except for in Georgia.

Georgia can thank Italy, and specifically Italian winemaker Josko Gravner, for spreading the word. When Gravner traveled to Georgia, he was fascinated by the qvevri and bought some for his winery in the part of Friuli close to the border with Slovenia. After initial experiments he was taken with the results. He ditched his wooden barrels and transferred his entire production into clay pots, which, much to the anguish of the Georgians, he called *anfora*. But not all *anfora* are created equal. The Spanish had *tinaja*, the Italians and Romans had *amphore* and *giare*, and the French had *dolia*. But the qvevri — originating from the Fertile Crescent — were the oldest of all of them. And they had a twist.

Built solely as subterranean fermentation and storage devices, they were one vessel for multiple purposes. Even if Gravner called them *anfora*, they were still qvevri. The wine he made in them was pricy juice that fetched over one hundred dollars a bottle.

On a practical level, what do winemakers find so appealing about them other than their romance and history? Gravner had this to say: "The ground has all the life you need to give birth to grapes. A vine needs the earth to make a grape. Once you have that grape, you need the earth again to make the wine." If your intent is to make natural wine—and these days the move toward natural is gravitational—the qvevri is a natural.

Conventional wine can be made in anything—food-grade plastic, cement, glass, wood, stainless, a bathtub, a tin cup, and, of course, clay. But no matter what the container of fermentation, conventional wines—the kinds that are mostly out there on the shelves—are allowed to have up to seventy-two perfectly legal additives. These include external yeasts and bacteria, enzymes, tannin, acid, gum arabic, uric acid, tartaric acid, fruit juice concentrate, and anti-foaming agents. Machines are available to reduce water and alcohol, change texture, and what not. All of these are undesirable to those committed to drinking naturally, as well as anathema to those wines that work to express their natural place and vintage. Those additives are aimed at making wine taste a certain way.

Then there's the issue of added sulfites. These are a natural by-product of fermentation, but adding sulfur dioxide as an extra preservative and antibacterial is commonplace. In the United States the legal limit is 350 parts per million (ppm), a measure that would most often be used for sweet wines; in dry wines the usage is closer to 200 ppm. A natural winemaker might add a little sulfite—20 ppm perhaps—very much different from the conventionally allowed limits. Even the addition of organic sulfite is huge at 100 ppm. Excessive sulfitage is detrimental. To my palate additions can snuff the life out of a wine. A winemaker who works without these additives feels like his or her job is to *shepherd* the wine through the fermentations and into the bottle. Using the commercial techniques and additives, the conventional winemaker *coerces* instead.

For shepherding, the qvevri has its fans. Traditional winemaking in

Georgia is done in the following way: grapes are usually foot stomped and slightly crushed into a hollowed-out log and flow into the qvevri by gravity. Alcoholic fermentation kicks off naturally. Punchdown, done with a primitive-looking wooden pitchfork, is done twice a day to push the grape skins down to keep them wet. Usually the second fermentation, malolactic fermentation, which converts the hard, tart acids into the milky, softer acids, happens far more easily and with more certainty in qvevri. Once the cap falls — this indicates fermentation is done — the grape solids are removed from the red grapes. The whites are left in their skins and stems. This step is called "leaving the wine with its mother," as it is getting all the nutrients it needs from the skins and the fine lees, the good bits left behind by fermentation, while the bad lees and the seeds fall into the nipple at the bottom of the qvevri, where they have limited touch with the rest of the wine. When fermentation is finished, a stone lid is placed over the top of the qvevri. This lets a tiny amount of oxygen in. In the spring, when the warmer weather comes, the qvevri is opened and the contents are moved with perhaps a pump (but more likely any number of shapes and sizes of low-tech gourds attached to sticks) into a freshly cleaned qvevri for storage until bottling; this is called "putting the wine on its feet." The little wine has grown up.

The first and foremost important advantage of a qvevri is its natural and mostly consistent temperature control, essential for healthy and easy fermentations. The second is its egg-like shape, which is viewed as mystical but also functional. For one thing, the shape aids gentle circulation and naturally clarifies the wine. For another, the material aids in micro-oxygenation, the slightest bit of exchange with oxygen. This kind of winemaking is called "reductive"; it might not promote fruity flavors, but it builds a wine to last.

What kind of clay and how pure it is are quite important factors. Giorgi had praised black clay. Clay can bring nutrition to some wines and allow for flavor development as well. The head oenologist for the Alaverdi Monastery Winery published a paper, "The Remarkable Qvevri Wine." In it he noted that some qvevri, made from "black earth and salty soils, are marked with a high concentration of zinc.

[The zinc] helps to increase sugar and the accumulation of aromatic substance." It certainly would seem to help retain a wine's aromatics, always beneficial in wine. I couldn't wait to get on the road. Black earth, here I come.

It's impossible to write about qvevri without writing more about the use of skin contact, for which Georgia is famous. How much skin contact the wine gets tends to differ by region in Georgia. Longer skin contact is more common in Khaketi in the east, and the result is in the color, texture, and flavor.

White wines in this way are slightly touched with the flavor of almond, walnut, and dried apple. Moreover, the long maceration in contact with grape seeds confers nourishing anthocyanins and useful properties. Amber, tea, sunset, venom, orange: no matter what you call the color, the idea of making a white wine like a red wine is nothing new. And anyway, eight thousand years ago probably no one was fermenting wine separately; all grapes, red or green, were thrown in together in a field blend. It made sense. Skins provide protection from degradation. They add structure and tannin. The question isn't why people have resurrected this way of making wine; more appropriate is why did they ever stop? The Georgians never did, but it took a while to explain it to the world.

Once Gravner started to experiment with the qvevri vessels, the trend spread to Slovenia and Austria and Croatia. Skin contact, which had been a lost tradition in the area, was revitalized. And whether they are made in a pot, a barrel, or in glass and whether they are a fad or just another option, skin contact wines are currently made in Spain, the United States, Canada, Australia, New Zealand, Chile, and South Africa. In seeking how to work with the skin and the vessel, there's been a never-ending galloping of the world's winemakers to the mecca of Georgia, paying homage to the place of wine and qvevri birth.

Gravner might have introduced qvevri and orange wine to a new drinker, but as soon as Georgia reemerged on the scene, the Georgians stole their tradition back. Orange wine and qvevri wine are now if not mainstream, at least another option in the tastes and flavors of wine and one that particularly appeals to those working naturally.

The summer after Thierry Puzelat started to import Georgian wines into France, he made his first visit to the country and toured around with John Wurdeman. From everything I heard, it was an epic trip, with very little sleep, some required wrestling, and a black eye or two. But while it looked like he was busy having fun, Puzelat was taking it all in—and not just the wine. He was moved. "It made me feel that I was a high interventionist," he told me. And that's why he and ten other high-profile French winemakers put in their order for qvevris for the 2013 vintage.

At one time there were hundreds of qvevri potters around the country, but they fell out of favor in Soviet times—the qvevri are not easy to care for, and as a result, they hindered productivity. So the craftspeople focused on what was seen as more useful work. Those masters who still held the knowledge and skill to make the vessels died out. By the time John took me to meet Zaliko, there were only three remaining masters, and Zaliko was at the top of the heap.

It's a long and interesting road, dry and almost like desert when one is heading out to Imereti in the west, but once through the Soviet-built tunnel, the Rikoti, it's lush. Town after town has something to sell; one village showcased tennis-racket-sized sweet breads. Another had foragers with baskets. "When it rains, the foragers are out here for Caesar mushrooms; ever had them?"

John and I share a passion for fungi. "Cook them [the Caesar mushrooms] in a clay pot, sizzle them up," he said as his eyes glazed over with adoration. "Porcini don't come close." But it had been too dry for mushrooms, and the peasants were probably picking early summer cherries instead. Then came the indication we were closing in on our mission as stall after stall of potters' crafts popped up. They were stocked with *tchotchas* and functional items, wine beakers, clay dishes, and clay ovens. Finally we pulled up on the road's shoulder and walked up on the grass toward a small collection of low-slung buildings. Here was Zaliko, one of the most sought-after qvevri makers in the world. To those wineries clamoring for qvevri, he was a life changer. He is a ruddy faced, compact man who, thanks to decades of working his clay, has the muscular arms of a man decades younger. Taking a break from working against the clock to make those qvevris, he was beaming with joy, a veritable sunflower as he came to greet us. After all, he had gone from believing that his craft was on a death watch to seeing it fully thriving almost overnight.

Zaliko had won life's lottery. He had gone from spending most of his time in his potter's studio making bread ovens, *pialas*, and baking dishes to making qvevri full time. He had gone from believing the plug was being pulled from his profession as a qvevri maker to an enviable three-year waiting list for one of his masterpieces. I was excited to see his workshop, where he fashioned the essential qvevri vessel, which has miraculously been saved from extinction to become Georgia's sexiest international export.

The air in his workshop smelled like fresh, sweet earth. The darkened room was crammed with qvevri of varying shapes and sizes in different stages of creation. The excitement was palpable, maybe because of the energy it took to work on the huge French order. For the 2013 vintage, France was going Georgian, and Zaliko had the commission.

But whether for Georgia or for France, the vessels are made the same way. The base with the point is thrown on a wheel, and after it gets to an ungainly size, the pot is then coil built. Seeing I was eager to observe his method, Zaliko grabbed a heavy rope of the local clay, dug from just above his home. It was something like a thick sausage. He laid it on top of a qvevri in progress. It was as high as Zaliko's chest.

"This one is two hundred liters and will take me fifteen days to complete," he said, starting to build the qvevri, which was completed up to the curve of its neck. He laid snakes of clay on top of it and with a primitive slat of wood blended the coils together seamlessly. Each rope had to dry for three days before he could lay the next one down. "The ones over there," he said, motioning to qvevri several feet above his head, "are six hundred liters and take a month to build and a week to fire." There was no use of a mold, no form. This was mastery of a plump, sensual creation angled, shaped, and built by his own hands. One man. One qvevri.

"And the clay," I asked. "Does it matter where it comes from?"

Without pausing he said, "The best is from here."

Of course. I didn't expect him to say anything else, especially if he didn't have a choice. His local clay was the only option.

Looking at the beauties before they were fired, I ran my hands over the still damp clay of the work in progress. I remembered one reason why the Soviets had scorned qvevri. They were too difficult to keep clean, something essential to making natural wine. I said, "But they are very difficult to clean; how should cleaning be handled?"

Zaliko dismissed my concern. "It's not so hard. You just scrub with a mix of lime and ash after fermentation. And beforehand, burning sulfur papers to make sure the qvevri is clean is the standard."

But it's not just that. It's tedious work, and few want to take it on. I remember Iago Bitarishvili, one of the "natural" guys, talking about how difficult it was to find people to help him do the cleaning. He had just finished his new winery, modest with twelve qvevri. The grapes were about to come in, and he was in a panic. "I go down to the village and I ask the men and the boys to help. I offer to pay them. Money! But no one wants to work," he said dejectedly. I looked at the person I was with, Jeremy Quinn, an American sommelier from Chicago who had decided to move to Georgia to change his life. "Here he is; here's your guy," I said, offering up Jeremy for the task. To my surprise, Jeremy was totally into it.

To show him what he was in for, Iago jumped into wellies, snatched a hose and a stiff horsehair scrub brush, and lowered himself down into the qvevri, as if it were an iron lung. With one hand he watered its interior and with the other, in very methodical fashion, scrubbed from side to side, getting in every crevice, essential so that no bacteria are able to form (or their presence could give a terrible mouse-like quality to the wine). Jeremy said, "That's no problem!" Iago had his extra pair of hands.

Those hands learned to use the winery tools as well. To scrape out the inside of a qvevri one uses a wad of cherry bark that looks like some sort of porchetta, preferably on a long stick.

Zaliko donned a little embroidered hat, a traditional one like a squat, modified festive fez, and guided us to his kiln. The kiln was actually a shack only a few meters away from his workshop, and it was tiny for its function — the size of my Manhattan kitchen. In there he built a wood fire that varies between 900 and 1,000 degrees Fahrenheit. The method is a bit cumbersome; for each firing he must build a brick wall to seal in the heat. Then the qvevri are fired. It can take a full week until they take on the glow of heat, and then they have to stay there until they cool down. To extract the vessels Zaliko must actually break down the entire wall and retrieve the pots. John told me, "When they are warm out of the oven, that's the time to coat and seal the inside with the propolis." Propolis is the resinous mixture that honeybees collect from tree buds, sap flows, and other botanical sources. It must come from a super pure forest. If it does for a qvevri what it does for my throat when I feel a cold coming on, it's a very good idea. And accordingly the substance acts as an antiseptic, falling into the pores and cleansing them.

A whole lot of qvevri were about to be shipped to France. Zaliko had sold plenty of qvevri to Europe, but the fact that so many prominent French winemakers had ordered from him made him stand taller and prouder. And just a few years ago he had been convinced that his beloved craft would die when he did. His sons were ready to dump their heritage for other fields. But now the qvevri and qvevri wine-aging method had been recognized by UNESCO's World Heritage Organization as a symbol of intangible cultural heritage. With winemakers around the world knocking on his door, as well as more commercial Georgian winemakers expanding their work with qvevri, the future for the fruits of his labor seemed robust. "I am the best in the country," he said, and it wasn't a boast from an egoist. "I've been doing this for fifty years; I can make these blindfolded. My sons are twenty-four, twenty-seven, and thirty. They make good qvevri but not as good as mine — as I constantly remind them. This craft is in my blood. People can try to do it, but you must love the qvevri first," he said. "I express my love to my country by building them. I create the environment for bread and wine. May you never have a lack of bread and wine," he said as a farewell, and went back to building those France-headed qvevri.

It had started to rain; we left in search of the peasants with mushrooms, and I couldn't help but feel excitement and sadness in one moment as I remembered what Giorgi had told me: "For thirty years there was no demand," he had said. "But now there is some life. In Imereti, there are Zaliko's sons. But when the old men die, how many new ones will take their place? That's the question."

WEST GEORGIAN LOBIO (BEANS)

Lobio encompasses all manner of beans (including string) and is a king in Georgian cuisine. You'll find *lobio* stuffed into breads and in salads and, like these, cooked up in a clay pot. Traditionally the dish is served with *mchadi*, which is quite similar to a puck of fried polenta, but frankly I prefer the beans with good, dense bread.

The technique here is to mash the herbs, onion, and garlic with the spices. Muddling fresh herbs for cooking was new for me, but it's superb. Svaneti salt, a salt/spice mix that comes from the Svaneti Mountains (a rural, pristine area in the most northwestern part of Georgia), could be used in place of the herb, onion, and garlic mixture, but it would not be traditional. In fact, it would theoretically be used only in Svaneti. If you can't acquire Svaneti salt, pick up some Moroccan or Indian seasoned salt or try mixing up some for yourself. A recipe for Svaneti salt follows.

Addiction warning: this is a highly soul-worthy recipe.

2 cups of dried pinto or red kidney beans

3 bay leaves

Svaneti salt

1 bunch of fresh green coriander

1 large onion

3 cloves of garlic

2 pinches of dried coriander

2 teaspoons dried blue fenugreek

1 teaspoon black pepper

1 teaspoon wild oregano, thyme, or fresh mint

3 tablespoons oil

Soak beans in cold water for 2 hours prior to cooking. Drain water and add beans, bay leaves, and salt to a deep pot containing 4 cups of water or at least 3 inches of water over the beans.

Bring to a boil and then lower to medium heat until the beans are tender.

Meanwhile, chop the fresh coriander, onion, and garlic, and grind the rest of the dry and fresh spices and herbs with a pestle or (as I have done) in a food processor.

Fry the onion in a pan of hot oil.

Drain the water from the cooked beans but reserve 2 cups of the liquid to use later. This is important, and don't forget it!

Use the back of a wooden spoon and mash the beans against the side of the pot. Add the ingredients that were crushed in a mortar. Add the fried onion. Mash.

Now mash all ingredients until completely mixed and add the reserved bean water. Transfer the ingredients to a pot and cook on medium heat for 4-5 minutes, stirring occasionally.

SVANETI SALT

2 heaping teaspoons dried coriander
1 heaping teaspoon dried dill
1 heaping teaspoon blue fenugreek
1 heaping teaspoon dried red pepper
1 heaping teaspoon dried marigold flowers
½ teaspoon dried caraway seeds, crushed
6½ teaspoons good coarse salt
1 bulb garlic

Mix the dried ingredients and then pulse with grinder or mix garlic in with fingers as if playing with sand on the beach. If you add crushed red chili it becomes a Megrelian variant. If you add water and cilantro it becomes Megrelian *adjika*. Put in ball jar for two days. You're done.

CHAPTER 4

WINE AND GOD

There is always a clash between idealists and pragmatists, gnostics and agnostics, those who live on instinct and those who dismiss it. That was evident as I sat with colleagues in the chapel that is the religious heart of the Alaverdi Monastery. It was during the First International Qvevri Symposium when a scientist from Germany took her place at the podium to deliver her talk. The problematic part of her discourse was when she held forth on the wisdom of using laboratory yeasts and enzymes to make wine.

The scientist was of the same mind-set as any scientist consulting to wine companies and recommending such additions to help make a more secure, dependable product, additions that quicken the process and ease the juice through fermentation in a more predictable way. The talk, which came off as dangerous and threatening to the very core of natural qvevri wine, provoked a rustle of emotion from the audience.

Alaverdi Monastery is a majestic presence nestled into the shadows of the purple Caucasus. Bishop Davit, metropolitan of Alaverdi, the very same Bishop Davit who had given his blessing for John to marry Ketevan, is its spiritual leader. Earlier in the day he had stood at the podium and welcomed us into his monastic home. He cut a profound figure with his wiry long beard, his black clerical robes, and his searching eyes full of—was that mischief? Yes. It must have been. For one thing,

I knew there was an iPhone in his pocket. I also knew that before he had turned to God and spent a decade living in caves in devotion, he had had a life studying architecture, living with his wife, an actress; there were even children. But then he had embraced celibacy as he delved deeper into religion and his own special preservation of ancient arts, including wine.

Wine for him was transportational and ultimately intrinsic to the church. When he had arrived at Alaverdi, entrusted with resurrecting it, he had discovered that making wine was an intrinsic part of its history. During the rebuilding of the monastery, excavations had unearthed an outstanding cellar of old qvevris of different sizes dating back to 1011. In 2006, the year before John and Gela started their winery, the bishop started Alaverdi's. He did this with funding from one of the country's largest wineries, Badagoni. Unlike what the bishop advised John to do — that is, make wine in qvevri — the winemakers at Alaverdi initially made wine both in qvevri and in barrels. But now that's changed. History and preservation of ancient arts is essential to the bishop, and the winery now concentrates on wine made from the buried vessels. And on the label is the notation, "Since 1011."

The monastery has also acquired vineyards and planted its own vines where previously it had bought the grapes. On its website it links its wine to God: "Since ancient times till now the Alaverdi Monastery wine has carried the praise to God. Wine heals the soul and the flesh, gives strength to thank the Creator, and brightens your mood; enjoy and share the splendor of Georgian royalty and the glory of the monks' modesty."

The bishop has made traditional and natural wine a mission of the church — so much so that he saw the need to sponsor a conference. He explained: "The church and wine are intertwined because you can't conduct a service without wine — a symbol of Christ's blood." But that doesn't begin to convey the amount of commitment it took to plant vines, resuscitate the wine cellar, and try to establish a school to further the traditional arts. After all, the Catholic Church has sacramental wine, and the Vatican has an extensive wine cellar, but the idea that a religious order would support a wine conference is quite a stretch.

Wine is essential to Judaism. It's blessed and sipped on the Sabbath and at every important ritual, such as circumcision and marriage, but were the vines ever essential to the culture and would rabbis ever see it as essential to support a wine conference to keep their tradition alive? No. But there I was in the midst of drinking monks and bishops. They were enjoying and (most of all) preserving the ancient traditions.

During the commotion the German scientist had created after discussing yeasts, arms shot up. And one hand shot up before the others. It was that of the oenologist for the monastery's winery. The man, who bore something of a resemblance to a more kindly Gorbachev, came to his feet. I saw he was proudly wearing traditional garb; a sword rested on his hip. He started to speak, and his voice shook with emotion. He attacked the researcher as if she were a heretic. "Are you saying that God did not provide the grape with everything it needed to make wine? There are no bad yeasts."

This "We are all God's children" approach to winemaking was new to me. While I tend toward the agnostic, I was impressed that this man believed in the concept of the balance in nature as being close to God. Start with healthy grapes. Embrace all of the yeasts, including those that initially give off flavors and funky aromas. After all, in any community you need diversity to create the whole in the most complex way. I had absolutely never heard a religious argument for making wine naturally, and it was nothing short of thrilling. Others thought so too. The man was given resounding applause.

So where did this connection between religion and wine in Georgia come from? I certainly see wine as spiritual, but in Georgia it is so deeply embedded into this deeply religious country that it is almost knit into its theology.

The Georgians were once deeply pagan, and the cult of Dionysus was rampant by the time Christianity came in. That's when, in the first half of the fourth century, Saint Nino was visited by the Virgin Mary, who gifted her with a grapevine saying, "By the strength of this cross, you will erect in that land the saving banner of faith in my beloved Son and Lord."

The belief is that the young Nino cut the vine in two, lopped off her long braid, and used it to plait the vines into a cross. Then she carried it with her along with the gospel to Georgia (Kartli or Iberia, as it was called back then), where it became a symbol of survival. There are persistent stories about soldiers in ancient times. Before they went into battle, a piece of vine was threaded into their chain mail and tucked close to their hearts. When a soldier went down, not long after the point of death, the grape vine started to grow, straight through the aorta. Life ends and life begins. This is the kind of apocryphal story that surfaces, whether it is a date tree growing through the heart of an Israeli soldier or a grapevine in ancient Georgia. It speaks to the emotions of the people (and even to me, through my own penchant for cynicism).

Zedashe is what the Georgians call sacramental wine. Where church wine is historically awful, in Georgia it was supposed to be the purest and the highest quality. In most traditional wineries there was always one qvevri dedicated to sacramental wine and intended for donation to churches, as well as for use during holidays. It was Giorgi Barishivilli who told me that making *zedashe* required special care, with more stirring while fermentation was going on. Also it was only red wine; a blending of the grapes was not allowed — a prescript that makes me wonder if it was religion that originally brought in the concept of separating the red grapes from the white — even though it took centuries and modern marketing to make it a booming trend. The old way, worldwide, had been wine from a blend.

The Catholic Church has a long history of protecting the vine. The most famous example is that of the medieval monks of Burgundy, who carefully mapped out their vineyards and realized what should be planted where. They tended the vines, they made the wines, and they also banished grapes they felt didn't belong on northern Burgundy soil.

But Georgia took its devotion to wine to another level and did so a whole lot earlier.

On several occasions I took the twenty-minute drive from the city of Telavi to the Ikalto Monastery, more to soak in the memories of the past (it had once been a thriving center of thought) than for any connection to religion.

Outside the cloister are the requisite craftspeople selling religious icons or prayer beads. Inside it was lush and wild. Built in the sixth century, the monastery became a cultural and intellectual center, not only for Kakheti in eastern Georgia but also for the entire country. In addition to courses on enlightenment, philosophy, astronomy, and, of course, theology, there were courses in crafts, chanting, and, yes, winemaking. It was where the poet Shota Rustaveli is believed to have studied. I love walking through the peace, through the neglected qvevris, moss covered and abandoned.

In its day each monk was allotted a hefty amount of wine per day for drinking. But in 1616 the Iranian invaders, led by Shah Abbas II, devastated the area, sacked Ikalto badly, and burned the church. The school ceased to exist, though the site remained a tiny if important house of worship.

Today it is tended by Father Zakari and his parish, under the leadership of Bishop Davit. People come to this place, where the wind always seems to gently blow, to soak in the peace and contemplate in the sweet chapel. Ikalto is evidence of a once-thriving wine culture in the extensive series of ancient qvevris.

The revival of Alaverdi as an icon of culture has become a passionate project for Bishop Davit. The idea is to make this a center for the teaching of traditional winemaking and qvevri making, as it once was. As the bishop told me, "Everything that man does with his hands is guided by God. If not the church, who will represent the past?"

To "represent the past" is one of the best purposes of religion that I'd ever heard. Perhaps that's why the bishop allowed his young monk winemaker, Father Gerasime, to travel to France, England, and Italy to show the monastery's wines at tastings in very unlikely settings for monks. Such was the case at the London Real Wine Fair, when a troupe of Georgian natural winemakers came for their very first time.

Father Gerasime is a beautiful man with sleepy eyes and a peaceful demeanor that belies his thoughtfulness and intensity. After he had showed the wines for hours at the fair, cutting a dashing figure in his black robes, we headed out to find some food and found ourselves near midnight in an Indian restaurant. As I sat beside him, so close to the black scratchy wool of his robes, I thought about that garb and its purpose. Was it not a little bit like a qvevri? Doesn't the use of the qvevri free up the ego from winemaking in the same way the robes free up clergymen from the ego of dressing and presenting themselves to the world in accordance with someone else's desire? Yes, he said, that was it exactly.

I then asked him if he had always been certain he wanted to give up worldly connections and devote himself to God. He told me he had always been sure he wanted the monastic life, except for one reservation: his burning desire to make wine.

His family had always vinified, and he felt that, second to God, making wine was his lineage and another kind of calling. Father Gerasime told me that his father's favorite activity was vine and wine. "He was never happier than when he made others happy. He never let guests from the city go without wine. If he was going to the city, he always took wine and other products from the village. He could play Georgian folk instruments; he sang traditional Georgian songs. We rarely had a week without guests. I was brought up in such a hospitable family. I helped my father as much as possible. After his death I felt obliged to continue that love and tradition. I took his grafting knives and started to graft vines and make wines. I took care of the vineyard and made wine in qvevri."

He started the ecclesiastical life. The priest who took his confession tasted the young man's wine and liked it so much that he was given the task of making the Church's wine. "This lasted three years, until I decided to go to the monastery."

When he entered Alaverdi as one of its novices, a devoted man who would live there, keeping up the monastery and deepening it as a religious center, Father Gerasime kept his craving to make wine a secret, as he saw no possible outlet for his desire. Alaverdi has been coming to life in the twenty years since the fall of Soviet rule, and with it so has a winery in the tradition of long ago. Father Gerasime said, "One day, a few years back, the bishop called me in to see him. He told me I would be in charge of the winery. I was silent for a long time, and the bishop said, 'You have to speak up. Are you happy with this decision?' I was speechless because it was what I had wanted to do my whole life. But I was sure I was going to have to sacrifice it when I became a monk."

Father Gerasime's face took on a beatific glow as he sat with his fork about to go into a chunk of *mattar paneer*. Like so many events in Georgia, his seemed ruled by fate.

"The vine requires hard work, care like for a child, and gentle treatment," he said. "Wine must be made wholeheartedly, with love, in the hope for God's grace. Wine shall be drunk at weddings, at a son's birth, at a funeral repast, to receive guests, for the joy of heart, as a gift to God and glory. Our bishop says, 'Wine for me is a strength in belief, inspiration in the love of my homeland, a force and firmness in the battle. Wine is everything for us—conscience, truthfulness, fairness, and courage.'"

Many religions have wine as a symbol; in the religion I was born into, Judaism, there is no *shabbos* meal or celebration without wine for a blessing—from weddings to births. There are strict rules on how to grow grapes and how to make wine. Certain holidays must be marked by wine, as in Passover, when four cups must be drunk at the seder. In some instances towns made it exclusively, such as Sagrantino, which was the sacramental wine for Umbria. Yet nowhere in the modern world is there a nation like Georgia, with this concept of wine—a fire coursing through its veins—as well as a place so close to God.

DANDURI

The nuns did the cooking during the conference, and good cooks they are. This is where I first encountered *danduri*, purslane. Purslane is a lemony wild green that grows out of the cracks of New York City sidewalks and in organic vineyards in Georgia everywhere. This recipe is just another showcase for never-ending variations of walnut sauce, and you can try it with any green—wild creeping purslane, spinach, or lamb's quarters. But purslane is particularly fine for this recipe, as it is so firm that it maintains texture.

> 1 pound purslane
> 3 tablespoons white wine vinegar
> ½ bulb garlic, finely chopped
> 1 cup ground walnuts
> handful of cilantro
> 1 teaspoon ground coriander seeds
> 1 teaspoon blue fenugreek
> ¼ teaspoon cayenne pepper powder
> 1 teaspoon marigold flower powder
> 1 tablespoon lemon juice (or to taste)
> salt and pepper to taste

Cut the purslane into 3- to 4-inch pieces. Blanch for 1 minute in boiling water, then put in cold water and then drain. Blend the vinegar and garlic together. Take 1 heaped tablespoon of the garlic and vinegar mixture and add to the walnuts and the remaining ingredients. Blend together using a mortar and pestle; add lemon, salt, and pepper to taste. Slowly add boiling water until it is a thin paste/thick sauce. Mix with the purslane. Chill.

CHAPTER 5

THE DREAMERS

The morning my great winemaker handoff kicked off—I was going to visit a number of wineries and winemakers throughout the country—I was sitting on the steps of Soliko Tsaishvili's house, drinking strong Turkish coffee with the smoking winemaker. Soliko was grizzled and missing a few teeth; it was a look that worked magnificently on the gruffly handsome man. Above us a pomegranate tree was resplendent with its firm, waxy, sunset-orange bell-like blossoms. And around us his place was a lovely mess. A rotted-out, miraculously still functioning Zaporozhets, the emblematic car of the Soviet era, was parked between the house and the winery, where the qvevri were buried.

I had met Soliko during that first conference at a nighttime wine tasting outside of the National Museum. I looked at his wine label, which reminded me of the 7 of Cups in the Tarot deck. That card was about letting go, a wild energy, and it was exactly how his Rkatsiteli, under the label Our Wine, tasted.

Morning was turning into sultry afternoon. Before I lost my concentration to the inevitable endless afternoon of food and drink ahead, I aimed to find out how Soliko, the first of the new Georgian winemakers who worked naturally to export his wines to the rest of the world, had started.

"Ah," he said, "for that we have to go back to the 1970s and 1980s, when the only kind of wine you could find was the shit made by the state." He was referring to the kind of wine cranked out by state "factories," such as the lumbering Factory No. 1 in Tbilisi. Built as a state-of-the-art winery in the 1880s, it was coopted by the Soviets in the occupation of the 1920s. For quite a while that huge factory was known to make relatively good wine.

I was familiar with the factory. Niki had brought me to see it. Then vacated, it was being turned into perhaps some sort of museum or restaurant, but it was still intact with many of the past relics: huge brass chandeliers, gorgeous deep woodwork, and massive mantles. It was an important setting for *Falling Leaves*, the 1966 wine-based movie of innocence and corruption by Georgia's most important filmmaker, Otar Iosseliani. Iosseliani filmed most of the action there.

"Especially in the late eighties" Soliko said, "toward the fall of communism, the wine was absolutely poisonous."

All of this poison started in 1928 with the first of Stalin's five-year plans. Stalin strove to reach the state's economic goals in five years through collectivization and industrialization. For agriculture that meant that private land was seized for the greater good of the state. Until the end of communism there would be no more farmers who worked for themselves. Households, not individuals, were allowed to retain one thousand square meters — about half a hectare — for household use; as a result, they were forced to squeeze as much as they could out of the earth, and squeeze they did. Plots were turned into multiuse projects growing their essentials — corn, tomatoes, cucumbers, eggplants, and grapevines. While commercial wine was the domaine of the state, households could make some for their own use. If a person longed for a career in wine, he or she could have it only in dreams.

By the time of the fall of communism in 1990, the Soviet Union had implemented eleven different five-year plans. But the real damage to wine started in 1971 with the ninth plan. That was when the demand for production was ratcheted up to the untenable. Wine quality plummeted. By the 1980s, according to Soliko, it was deplorable. Only if one could make one's own or get homemade wine could a person drink good wine. It helped if one had connections.

"As always, everyone in the countryside still grew grapes and made wine in their wine cellars, and most people still used qvevri. They had it good. City people like me? We had it rough. I lived in Tbilisi. You had to pull some strings to find those who had some wine to sell to outsiders."

"It was a black market?" I asked.

The idea that there was a black market in something as innocuous as homemade wine was inconceivable. To acquire this rarity—good wine—Soliko and his friends asked other friends where they could acquire their favorite drink. Competition was fierce. They finally found a source in nearby Kakheti, but they couldn't buy enough to get them through the year, so they had to find a better solution: make their own.

After a slug of the muddy coffee, Soliko took a drag on his cigarette. The wind kicked up and blew his gritty smoke into my face. He continued the tale.

In 1988, three years before the Soviets left the country, wine was at its worst. The friends sourced grapes from Kakheti. They crushed the Rkatsiteli and Mtsvane and plunked the juice into glass demijohns. In the end they made about four hundred liters (about 105 gallons). The resulting wines were so much better than what was available that they drank the young wines and drank them all quickly. All were gone by February (they had most likely started drinking them the December before). "But at least we were happy for a few months." In 1989 there was a massacre in Tbilisi of protesters demanding the withdrawal of the Soviet Union; twenty were killed and two hundred wounded. That resulted in a radicalization of the Georgians. It was the beginning of mayhem: crime, poverty, and civil war. It didn't end in 1991, when Georgia declared independence. Starting with the fall of communism, there were three wars and a period of thirteen years where there was unreliable electricity and infrastructure. The crime situation was extreme. And while Georgians were eager for private business, no one knew how to go about starting it.

That's why, for years, instead of vinifying, Soliko told me, they needed to put all their energy into survival. Speaking slowly, he took long pauses as he gazed over my head into the past; he's not big on eye contact. As the decade rolled away from communism, hope trickled in. Georgians started to consider that peace and stability could be possible. That is when thoughts once again turned to the irrepressible vine.

"We first made Our Wine in 2003, in the true Kahketian way," he said, referring to the eastern tradition of long skin contact in wine. "Except we didn't have qvevri. Instead we made that first vintage in a big jug lined with ceramic tiles, like a huge swimming basin."

Encouraged by the results, the friends went further in fantasy toward reality. Why not form a cooperative winery with five friends, buy a small house in Kakheti, and then acquire some vineyards near where they had been buying those excellent grapes? "I'm a literature specialist," Soliko (who had been an academic) said. "My job was flexible. I didn't have to be in Tbilisi all the time. I could be here, taking care of the vines and the wines." He, unlike others who were from the country and yearned to take on the craft of the grandfathers, had found wine in a different way. He had fallen in love with it. Simple as that.

"That was the beginning. We thought we needed consultants to make really good wine." In what was a repetitive story with so many of the people I talked to, he added, "When we found them, they all talked yeast and sulfur. This is not what we wanted. We wanted to work with tradition."

Finally they found Gogi Tushmalishvili, the rare consultant who had his feet planted in the wisdom of the past. Zoliko said, "He would be ninety now. He told us because our vines were where they were, in the Kardanakhi and Bakurtsikhe viticulture micro-zones — historically known as the best terroirs — we had to make qvevri wines the old way."

The friends followed the old way of farming too, and in describing their work to me, Soliko showed his impatience. "No one should harm nature for profit. There's absolutely no excuse for it," he said.

Whether or not their methods stem from the religious conviction for purity, Georgians believe that the soil and wine need to be protected. The Soviets were famous for raping the earth, and they brought chemicals to the farmers to pump up production. But at home, in their own gardens, the Georgians mostly stayed organic. Pollute their own wine? Never.

Oddly enough, in France it was the chemicals that gave rise to the renaissance in natural winemaking. In the 1970s salesmen came around to rural French vineyards and propaganda sales started: winemakers needed additives to make wine, and they needed chemicals to work less in the vineyards. As a result, France went into one of the darkest ages of winemaking in its history, with bereft soils and bereft wines. There was a famous wine tasting in Paris in 1976, celebrated in a book called *The Judgment of Paris*, where California wine was pitted against the wine of France. California, shockingly, won. Because of a lack of attention in the French vineyards? Perhaps. At the time, one of the most destroyed areas was the Beaujolais. Unlike the Georgians, the French had willingly given up their birthright to making natural wines from healthy vineyards. As soon as they saw what was lost, they went in search of its revival. The natural wine movement took hold because in the late seventies a young man named Marcel Lapierre and his equally young friends were fed up with the poor quality of wine they were producing. They returned to organic, and they started to work minimally in the cellar. They were looked upon as hippie flunkies, but in the end their legacy triumphed; now, almost forty years later, natural wine is a brilliant success. Meanwhile, for the seventy years of communism, Georgia waited in the catacombs, waiting to celebrate its tradition as soon as it could.

As I sat next to Soliko, listening to his story, I had to draw the parallel between the Georgians' love for their wine and the poem *The Knight in the Panther's Skin*, in which two men — Avtandil and Tariel, a knight — who are bound in profound friendship for each other seek, through much adventure and danger, the object of Tariel's romantic love, the princess Nestan. How could I not see this whole modern-day Georgian qvevri tale as a search for the true love of wine? The devotion was just as passionate. As soon as liberation from the Soviets occurred, the search was on for how to make wine in the true Georgian way.

In another remarkable contrast and parallel, unlike in France, this return to the wine wasn't led by youth but by elders — or at least those in middle age.

When Gela Patashvili approached John Wurdeman, he was already thirty-three, an age that isn't ancient but is far from impetuous youth. Driving this wave of artisanal winemaking were those who had been forced to delay their dreams.

The age span of those managing the heavy lifting of change ranged from thirty to seventy. They were creating a vibrant showcase of wine from their country, promoting the organic as superior and offering the lack of additives as a serious alternative. They were gaining places on fancy wine lists, such as Denmark's Noma and Catalonia's Can Roca. The Georgian wine revolution against the chemical and the conventional did not belong to the youth.

Soliko suffered no fools, and in his opinion, to damage the earth was not only foolish but also demonic. He added another good reason to work naturally in the winery: "Georgians typically drink two liters a day, so it's important not to have chemicals that can cause hangovers. Not only that, but during the drinking there are fewer arguments, and the drunk is a softer, gentler drunk."

I wasn't sure about the fewer arguments or the softer, gentler drunks. I've seen my share of winemakers the mornings after, with their sheepish grins. I've seen crazy drinking. The Georgians are not shy, and just because it's not vodka, it doesn't mean the *kantsi* don't get passed around or the contents don't get glugged in one shot. It doesn't mean that the drinking doesn't get as out of hand as when there's vodka involved, but this I do know: the wines feel salubrious. They feel healthful in my body. But then, I don't often guzzle two liters of wine a day as a matter of course. I stick closer to half a bottle.

When even the faintest hint of government stability started to be possible, those waiting in the shadows to pounce on the new winemaking possibilities started to connect through the Georgian organic farming association, Elkana. They also met through Slow Food, the organization founded in Italy and dedicated to preserving traditional and regional cuisines and farming worldwide. The head of the Georgian Slow Food branch was the gravelly voiced Ramaz Nikoladze, who — no surprise — also made wine. When Soliko met Ramaz, he realized they shared the same values. Together they started to sniff out others who had the same passion to work in the old way, making excellent homemade organic natural wine, and who wanted to sell it in the marketplace. Acting as wine missionaries, they pieced together what would become a serious network.

One link they discovered was Ramaz's uncle, Didimi Maglakelidze. He was past seventy when his face was first illustrated on a bottle emblazoned with the unlikely name for his wine, *I am Didimi from Dimi and this is my Krakhuna.* He was seventy when his first wine was sold commercially in Italy. Another link was also from the west coast of Imereti, Gaioz Sopromadze. He's a *khachapuri*-bellied man and, like many others, in his sixties. He is known for working with the Chavkeri grape on his rich soils.

Thierry Puzelat started bringing Gaioz's wines into France after discovering them on his first visit to Georgia. "It tastes like chicken ass," he said to Gaioz, with John translating. "I'll take it all."

No one was sure what chicken ass tasted like or if Thierry was referring to raw or cooked chicken ass, but it was true that in Gaioz's hand the grape did become kind of meaty. Gaioz was happy. Very happy. And he was thrilled to travel to France. In 2013 he went with the others to sell his wines at the Dive Bouteille, the tasting where I had first brought John and Gela. Gaioz was having a hard time refraining from pinching the derrières of the Parisian fairer sex, as if it were Italy in the 1960s. When John intervened and told him to behave himself, he protested; he told me, "But they are just so beautiful!" He was so innocent in his appreciation that it was almost possible to overlook the sexism. Later that week I met up with him and the other Georgians in the Loire, in a beautiful deep cellar packed with a library of vintages dating back to the 1920s. Gaioz was angry, and he spoke in Georgian, so John had to translate: "My grandfather had three hectares of vines. Everything was taken!" He said this with so much emotion that he could have been speaking of recent events instead of those in 1921. "They divided our homes. We were stripped of our land, and it was given to people who had no idea how to work it. They took our cellar. We had bottles just like here," he said, looking covetously at the vintage upon vintage in the Loire cellar. Then with a sneer he said, "I hate communism and Communists."

The older man gained a youthful zeal. In fact, Gaioz, who at the time owned only three-quarters of a hectare, started buying new vineyards. Planting new vines at his age? Planting vines he wouldn't see bear fruit for years? This was optimism of the most undying kind. But in Georgia, where spirituality runs deep, so does commitment to the long term. And if unconditional love and the power of friendship are themes in Rostevili's *The Knight in the Panther's Skin*, so they are for the Georgians and their vines.

Finally the smells of lunch plumed out of Soliko's house. The food started to be laid out on a table under a cherry tree. Nino, Soliko's wife, joined us and watched us exclaim over her culinary skill: fritters, mushrooms, and an egg dish that was made with eggs so flavorful, I mused that they must have come from some sort of magic chicken. So much of Georgian wine is drunk and finished before proper aging, but at that lunch we tasted vintages. Soliko held up the 2006 Rkatsiteli and said, "This is my love. This is me."

Four hours later we were just beginning to think about calling it quits. Lunch in that country easily blends into the next meal. Even though I felt fattened up like a calf, rest was not to be. I had another appointment.

Waiting to make my good-byes, I leaned on the doorpost and watched as Soliko helped Nino clean up — not a usual scene in the country. And as they did, they fell into song, hitting harmonies not heard in other countries, layered like sandstone. I realized that polyphony wasn't just for entertainment, provided by groups such as Ketevan's Zedashe, but also part of real life. The tunes and singing were in layers, just as the wine is in layers. This singing and poly-everything is integral to the warp and weft of life there.

In the winemaker relay, with me as the puck, Kakha Bershivili, who speaks not a word of English, took me back to his home. He brought along a friend of his daughter's, a young winemaker, who would translate for us.

Kakha was a vegetarian violinist who, as soon as he could, also became a farmer and winemaker. A believer in all things natural, he is another member of the "I'm-no-longer-young-but-I'm-leading-the-wine-revolution" team. We stopped off at the market in Telavi and walked down the steps into the bustle, immediately finding stalls where we could stock up on a kilo of mushrooms for dinner. It seemed as if everyone knew I loved mushrooms.

That night, after visiting Kakha's vines and winery and walking near the river, we settled into cooking and drinking on the porch. With the darkened night the jackals howled increasingly behind the cacophony of the frogs and spring insects. I've never heard insects so determined and insistent. On the edge of summer solstice, nature was in heat.

As we talked, I was increasingly becoming interested in the twenty-something translator. A winemaker, he hoped to be off to New Zealand and Burgundy for internships after his enology studies.

"Where do you want to work?" I asked.

He wanted a job in a big factory in Georgia or out there in the rest of the world.

"Really?" I was surprised. "But even after today, hearing the stories and drinking the wines, aren't you a little curious about knowing how to make wine this way?"

He laughed. He said he loved the wines and their taste but added, "It's just too much work."

"Too much work? Aren't you embarrassed in front of these men, who are decades older than you? They're not afraid of the work," I said.

But the boy had been brought up with relatively little struggle, having been born after the fall of the Soviet Union. He didn't know what it meant to have dreams deferred and then embrace them in middle age. I found myself almost as sad as I had been on that late night with Niki in Tbilisi, arguing with the man at the cooking school. Sure, it's hard to clean the qvevri, but who in Georgia is afraid of hard work?

"You just want it cushy," I chided him, and he good-naturedly laughed.

"You can get a job with a big factory, but would you be able to sleep well at night knowing you were making wine you didn't really want to drink? Wouldn't you rather make wine like Kakha's?" I asked, as we dove into some of the brilliant wines from 2009 and his first 2006. Drinking the old and the new, we dug into the mushrooms. Savoring the tomatoes, I worried about Georgia because if the next generation didn't continue the elders' labor, would industrial wine triumph? That would be a disaster.

NINO'S DELICIOUS CABBAGE FRITTERS

This recipe, so simple but so flavorful, gives cabbage nobility. It struck me that the fritters were reminiscent of vegetable latkes made in Eastern Europe. Though Nino said the recipe came from her head and was not traditional, in scouring through old cookbooks I came across many a fritter variation from mostly the western part of Georgia. Love the fresh tarragon. Serves four.

    ½ head cabbage
    3 carrots
    2 eggs
    ½ bunch fresh tarragon
    salt and pepper
    bread crumbs
    oil for frying

Boil the cabbage for 10 minutes. Let it cool and then squeeze it out. Then chop or pulse it in a food processor. Grate the carrots and add to the chopped cabbage.

Add eggs, chopped tarragon, salt, and pepper.

Coat with breadcrumbs to obtain thick mass and shape into fritters. Fry up in oil on both sides in a hot frying pan.

ADJIKA

Some call it the Georgian salsa, but I find that calling it the Georgian answer to Morocco's *harissa* is more like it. Nino's was particularly delicious.

½ cup walnuts
5 cloves garlic, peeled
1 large red pepper, cored and seeded
1 large celery stalk, including leaves
½ pound fresh hot red peppers, including seeds
3 teaspoons blue fenugreek
3 teaspoons dried coriander
3 teaspoons dried marigold flowers
2 teaspoons dill (fresh or dry)
1 teaspoon salt
⅓ cup red wine vinegar

In a food processor grind the walnuts and the garlic until you have a paste. Coarsely chop the celery, large red pepper, and fresh hot red peppers and add them to the garlic and nut paste. Add the chopped herbs and red wine vinegar and pulse to a medium coarseness. Adjust seasonings.

CHAPTER 6

STALIN'S LAST WINEMAKER

I was mesmerized by the sadness of a word: *bogano*. The old Georgian word references a pauper. But the meaning is far deeper; it can refer to a citizen without a nation, a writer without a pen, a farmer without land, a peasant without a vineyard. Maybe I just relate to being disenfranchised, but it is a word plump with emotion. After meeting so many of the silver-haired men who had been disenfranchised of their land, who searched for their métier as if searching for a lost love, I wanted to see the other side. I wanted to meet a winemaker who had actually worked under the Soviets. I wanted to talk to someone who had made wine when others couldn't, even if he was a pauper without land. So when I found out that I could meet an important elder statesman of the trade, I delayed all other trips, grabbed John to translate, and dragged him, not unwillingly, to the Wines and Vines institution in Tbilisi, where Givi Chagelishvili still works.

Givi's boss during the Soviet era had been Iosif Vissarionovich Dzhugashvili, the man who changed the world. He changed winemaking. Along the way he also changed his name to Joseph Stalin.

Born in the middle of Georgia in a town called Gori, Stalin grew up to become the feared leader of the Soviet Union. Ruling from 1923 until his death in 1953, though he helped to defeat Nazism, he was also responsible for the murder of millions and the establishment of the labor camps in Siberia. But his home country of Georgia had a special place for him. God knows why, they still love him. I could just hear it: "He was Georgian! He wasn't that bad!"

Maybe it's because he loved wine and made sure that even if individuals could no longer make it, the state would make enough for his grandiose needs. Yet by wrenching land away from individuals and collectivizing it into state property, he turned the country into one replete with *boganos.*

The Wines and Vines building was under construction, and a sturdy, compact man with snowy hair, a pink nose, and slate blue eyes stood in the doorway. He had an aura of stifled anticipation, as if he were greeting a daughter he hadn't seen in a long time but didn't want to show how much he had missed her. I wasn't flattering myself that this was personal; he, like most Georgians, believed that guests are sent from God. As John and I walked toward him, his hammy arms hung from his shoulders in a shrug as if afraid to embrace. Givi was eighty-six years of age.

The man ushered us into the future home of the National Wine Agency. The old building had inches of plaster dust everywhere and smelled of leftover lunch, cigarettes, and black tea. Off to the side was a Soviet-era television. A glowing hot plate, holding a deep, amber-colored tea that looked to be about a week old, sat on the floor. On the wall was a makeshift cross. On the way to Givi's desk I passed a bottle of wine with Stalin's face emblazoned on it and tried not to be too obvious as I stole iPhone shots of the label.

The elder statesman sat down behind his desk, folded his hands together, and eagerly told me the story about how the deadly dictator had been determined not only to ensure the country's productivity but also to make sure he had enough to drink and stock his cellar. There might have been a five-year plan, but Stalin had his own private plan and it was to get his drink on. Moldova and Georgia (especially) were his vineyards.

Givi finished school in 1950, around the same time as state recruiters came around to the Tbilisi oenology department. They were in search of a man who could be trusted. "The most important thing," he said, "was not whether I could make wine but who my relatives were. Those with relatives who had taken part in demonstrations or uprisings needed to be purged. I had the most innocent history. But it was scary. I knew that if one thing went wrong . . ." and here he made the gesture and sound of a throat being cut.

Historians may have reported truthfully or not that Stalin may have been an alcoholic and/or a manic-depressive, but he was certainly very particular. Givi said, "The wines we made for Stalin came from hand-selected bunches in specific micro-regions. The bottles came from Romania. The corks came from Portugal. As he was fearful of being poisoned, each winery that made wine specifically for the Kremlin had dedicated Stalin-only bottling rooms. Every week there were plane deliveries to Moscow. "These carried live sheep from one specific area in Imereti where the sheep, because of their grazing on salty grass, had a gentle aroma. Stalin also loved apples from one particular village. And along with the weekly food delivery, twenty-five bottles flew off every week to Moscow."

"One hundred bottles a month?" I said, thinking that given how much the Georgians drank, it didn't seem like very much at all.

He qualified, "Those were just for him alone."

There were also other wineries making wine for the leader, so the total quantity of wine could have been huge.

But while Stalin loved wine, it wasn't the only alcohol he was known to drink. In *A Brotherhood of Tyrants* D. Jablow Hershman wrote that Stalin started the day with a half pint of vodka at daybreak, another at lunch, and a bottle of wine at dinner. While he didn't cite how he knew about the vodka, Stalin's drinking games seem indisputable.

Hershman continued: "Stalin insisted that his guests keep up with his own consumption of alcohol." At Stalin's dinners, Khrushchev stated, "There were often serious drinking bouts. . . . I remember Beria, Malenkov, and Mikoyan had to ask the waitress to pour them colored water instead of wine because they couldn't keep up."

"And what kind of wine did he like?" I asked.

"He liked qvevri wine," Givi said, smiling and showing the glint of his gold dental work. "He especially liked Chinuri from near Gori, his hometown. Gori is in the middle part of Georgia, close to Ateni. These Atenuri wines were traditionally made in qvevri but without skin contact. Initially we used to bring the juice over from Ateni, but it didn't survive the journey. When the juice arrived in Tbilisi, it was spoiled. So Stalin built a factory right in the village to take care of it on the spot."

It turns out that Stalin also loved a grape I too looked out for, the Tavkveri. This dark grape, which can be leathery and floral at the same time, was endangered because of its low productivity. A female grape, it needs to be co-planted, usually with Chinuri, so that it can produce fruit. I found it ironic that Stalin favored grapes of quality that were in low production when all one could find in the markets at the time were Saperavi and Rkatsiteli.

I asked, "Were you ever worried about how your wine tasted? I mean, what if Stalin didn't like the wine? It could have been dangerous."

Givi shook his head slowly. "It was a very big responsibility." He paused, thought, and then continued: "One time I thought I had made a fatal mistake. After a delivery, a big black car came for me at my home. The men put me in the car and drove me away. I was panicking. Had one of the corks leaked? Had they not made the trip and been bad? These men were from the KGB. They weren't telling me anything. They had faces of ice. I was watching closely because I knew if they turned toward the headquarters, I was done. But when they didn't and took a different turn, I realized I was safe. They took the turn to the factory. They were just giving me another order. "Relief" wasn't strong enough a word. I was young when I became gray; they could have finished me off very easily."

After Stalin died in 1953, the private bottling plants were closed and Givi was shipped off to the west. First he went to Meskheti, and then after sixteen years of making wine there he was transferred to Batumi before finally coming back home to Tbilisi. The places he talked about were ones to which I hadn't yet been, nor had I ever tasted any wines from them. Both were wine areas that had achieved glory at one time but had faded. Givi told me that there were some grapes and some vines, if you knew where to look for them, beyond the state-approved ones and of historical interest. "In a small village, there is a vine that is over four hundred years old," he said. I was stunned. I had seen two-hundred-year-old vines in the Canary Islands, but four hundred? A vine that had seen the Turkish invasions and the Soviets and still bore fruit? Now that was a living piece of history that I longed to see.

Givi had been making wines for sixty-eight years — not quite four hundred, but long enough. He had seen the wine industry go from state-controlled to free, from a government that revered wine to one that almost desecrated it. "That film, *Falling Leaves*," I asked, "did you ever see it?"

The older man seemed to squint to try to remember. After all, he worked at the very factory that was depicted in that film. John started to jog his memory about Otar Iosseliani's first feature-length film. "*Giorgobistve*," John said, parsing the Georgian name for the film. The old man considered it, and then said, yes, he remembered: "Yes, I saw it. Shortly after it was screened, it was banned."

Did he like it, or was he too much of a party man? I couldn't figure it out.

The film was set in the Victorian-era Factory No. 1 in Tbilisi that I had visited. When I walked through I was impressed by its woodwork and flashy brass light fixtures, but the dazzling parts were the floors below the earth, where the enormous barrels had been kept; some of them were still there. Then there was a mystery behind lock and key: thousands of bottles, caked with mold, from the Soviet area, untouched, because for decades no one had known what to do with them.

I brought the film up because I wanted to know if its premise had a basis in truth. It was about a bumbling innocent boy who landed a job in the winery and unwittingly came across a plot to increase wine production by adulteration. The young idealist took a stand — but still didn't win the girl at the end. The film was banned in Tbilisi shortly after its debut in 1967, not so much because of its content but because of its symbolism. The tainted wine barrel was No. 49. As it was close to the fiftieth anniversary of the October Revolution of 1918 and as the color of wine involved was red, these were additional problems. However, in Russia these weren't problems, and Russia sent the film off to Cannes, where it was accepted for the festival. The filmmaker finally fled the country in 1984 in search of artistic freedom; he said that to him wine wasn't about drinking but about spirituality. "That's why drinking wine is so important in my films. It brings people together, helps them to discover something new—maybe even happiness." But that was after Stalin's time. It was under Leonid Brezhnev that the wine problems in the country multiplied. One of the changes was the qvevri's rapid demise.

"For a while making wine in qvevri became unpopular," Givi said. "It was a lot of work to clean them; if you don't have water, you have to bring it in from somewhere else. Villages have a poor water supply, and you need a lot of water to clean the vessels."

John solemnly chimed in, as if the qvevris were religious and scared icons. "After that time they were relegated for storage. Some were even destroyed beyond rehab after being used to hold diesel fuel."

The big problem here that John and Givi were talking about was the five-year plans, which were increasingly diluting Georgian quality. The final plan, with its draconian charges, pushed the limits of the vine for even more heroic yields.

"I remember the vivid scene in *Falling Leaves* where the young hero goes out to lunch with a group of workers," I said. "They saw a bottle of wine from their own factory and they refused to drink it."

"Yes," Givi said. "Things got worse. During Stalin's time we didn't use a lot of sulfur. We inoculated fermentations but with yeasts we cultivated ourselves. Now there are French yeasts, but we don't use them. We don't recommend them. When they are used, they give off a strange aroma. They're made to make the wine smell differently, and then wine loses all quality of variety."

But in 1972, even though they didn't use those French yeasts, Givi told me there were worse crimes against wine and man. "One worker was caught putting acetone in the wine," he said. "He was fired, and I replaced him."

Fired? That had to be a euphemism.

By the time Soliko and his friends started to make wine in the 1980s, the situation had become impossible.

I was blessed to have tasted some wines from the Soviet era. One night

John appeared with some mystery bottles with heavy, dense wax caps that struck me as odd. The caps were an artisanal touch, not something I would have associated with the Soviets. There was a 1961 Rkatsiteli, which I started to greedily drink. It was caramel, with brilliant acid and counterpointed with an earthy, intense walnut. There was a 1961 Mtsvane from Ikalto, not far from Alaverdi. This was a beauty—golden, emotional, with some ginger and mushroom. Then there was an interesting Saperavi from 1964—tomato juice, earth and clay, with quite a bit of nail polish remover. There was no indication that any were made in qvevri, most probably they were not, but they showed talent.

Givi said, "From the 1970s and '80s winemaking was pushed to over 45 percent of the potential yield of the '60s. But then, toward the end, to be profitable the state required even higher yields. But it was not possible. There's just so much a vine can give. To fulfill the five-year plan quotas they had to bring in sugar and Chaptalize to extend the product. That affected the taste. With all that sugar you need a lot more sulfur. It was one-half sugar and one-half sulfur."

Givi was animated; he might have been a winemaker for sixty-eight years, but he wasn't showing any diminished enthusiasm. After decades of seeing the qvevri disappear, it was back, and the wine it made was back. "A Chinese crew was even here to do a documentary!" he said with excitement.

When I asked him about the biggest change he'd seen, he said with pride, "Today people can make wine in qvevri with as much quantity and with as much or as little skin contact as they want. There is no recipe. You don't have to press the grapes as if you're wringing the water out of a rag to get every last drop. The wine is reverting back to the kind of wine we used to make—free run, full of juice and life. We are free."

These old men had a passion for wine that belied the drink, and it showed me where the Solikos, the Gelas, and the Nikis drew their passion. Wine was their birthright.

Givi walked us out into the sunlight. I had John take my picture with him. How could I not? Stalin's last winemaker! It was then he told me the secret of his stamina: "I drink wine every day and drink 100 grams of *chacha* every night."

LAMB CHAKAPULI

A *chakapuli* is a slow-cooked stew and can be made of anything, from veal to mushrooms. Lamb is the classic ingredient and was probably in the much-loved, even nostalgic dish that was prepared for Stalin from those live sheep fed on salty grasses flown to him from western Georgia.

What is *chakapuli* about? Celebration. The celebration of spring herbs and young lamb. It also relies on unripe plums, an essential element for the acidity. If you can't find the lovely sour kind, tart the stew up with lemon juice. There will be quite a broth; traditionally the meat is eaten first, and then the liquid is drunk as a soup.

    2 pounds diced lamb
    2 cups white wine
    ½ pound onions
    3 bunches tarragon (this is the most important herb for this dish)
    2 bunches cilantro
    1 bunch arugula or mint
    1 bunch scallions
    2 green spicy peppers—jalapeño or serrano but not
        green bell
    3 tablespoons chopped green garlic
    ½ pound wild sour plums (if they are really sour you'll have
        to leave the pit in)
    2+ cups water
    salt (according to taste)

Cover lamb with white wine and cook on a low heat until cooked through and the wine is reduced (usually 15-20 minutes). Stir occasionally with a wooden spoon.

While the meat is cooking, chop the onions, tarragon, cilantro, arugula, scallions, and peppers. Crush the garlic. Add the chopped ingredients, the garlic, and the sour plums to the cooking lamb. Add more water just to cover, and cook for about an hour. If you don't have the sour plums, or if they're not sour enough, use lemon juice to flavor or green *tkemali* sauce, which you can find in Georgian specialty shops.

CHAPTER 7

YOM KIPPUR
AND CHINURI

In the fall of 2012 my most recent book had been translated into Georgian. There was to be a big *supra* at the publisher's. Terrific. They were going to bring me over. Even better. The event was to be held, however, the day after Yom Kippur. I said no.

John said I needed to be there. He wasn't Jewish, and I wasn't sure he could understand.

"I know I'm not religious," I said to him, "but this is a day that is sacred. It is the Jewish New Year for the soul. I fast twenty-five hours. I don't use electricity of any kind. I don't get into cars. I don't socialize. I have to go to shul."

"There are Jews in Tbilisi, you know, and there are temples here as well."

I believe in ritual. I go hunting for ramps in the spring. I dance in the streets on May Day. I attend seders at Passover, follow the rules of what I cannot eat for the eight days of the holiday, and fast on Yom Kippur. Some things are just not negotiable. But I talked it over with my brother, who lived in Wisconsin. Andrew was an invasive cardiologist and didn't travel as I did, but he was entranced by my visits to Georgia. This country gripped his imagination. "Of course you have to go," he said. "It's work. And, I mean, who knew there were Jews in Georgia?"

Until that moment I had never strayed from my personal rituals on the Day of Awe in New York City. When I was a kid, I looked to it with dread, but oddly enough as I grew older and left an organized sort of religion, the day took on greater meaning as I found a way to make it my own way. This is what it looks like. I go to shul at dusk. I fast. I bang my chest. I go home. I return in the morning. I beat my chest some more. I think. I sit in the women's section, never questioning why I put up with the segregation. I return home. I sleep. In the morning I head back to temple. Come the afternoon break, I walk back to my bed, where I dream as if I've been smoking opium. I return at dusk. I contemplate Jonah and the whale. I contemplate the question of the day: Who shall live and who shall die? Who by fire, who by affliction? I sing "Avinu Malkenu." And then I wait, as people have for centuries before me, to hear the primitive blast of the ram's horn, the shofar, and finally the first morsel of bread and sip of wine.

But John was right. I could observe without compromises in Tbilisi as long as the organizers sprang for a hotel within walking distance of the Great Synagogue on Leselidze Street. "Fine. Let's do it," I told him. But then another explosion hit just two weeks before departure.

"I have cancer. And it's not good," my brother told me.

There was no cancer in my family. It was impossible. It couldn't be, but it was.

My first word as a baby had been "Ahdew," not "Mommy." My first memory was my brother lifting me from my crib. We were inseparable, way beyond the years I should have already become the annoying little sister. When I hitched away from home as a depressed teenager, it was directly to Andrew's dorm room. When I needed sex advice, I went to my brother. In trouble, he contacted me, even through dreams. He went on to marry, live in Milwaukee, have kids, become a cardiologist. I stayed single. He saved lives; I saved vines. We lived far away from each other, he in Milwaukee with his family, me with my wine books and bottles in New York City. I had always thought we would have time for each other later in life.

"What could be better than being here in Georgia with people who love you? Especially now?" John asked.

I love tradition but have little faith in prayer. That didn't change the work in front of me: I had a lot of heavy lifting to do in the spiritual department. But the thought of being so far away made me terribly nervous.

"Go," my brother said. "It's work."

We were both workaholics. Work in my family trumped everything. "Don't worry, I'll still be here when you get back."

He was, after all, just getting used to the idea of chemo pumps and poisons, putting together the passwords for his wife, ordering his life, holding out for the morsels of hope.

They did get me a hotel close to the temple. It was weeks before the election, and all of Tbilisi was being torn up as a last-minute bravado on the part of Mikheil Saakashvili to show that he could repave the tire-puncturing roads. My hotel was at the top of a hill all torn up with no access, and I had to carry my bag along the not quite finished street, where the workers were hand-layering-in cobblestones.

After a last meal with John at Ghvino Underground (the cooperative natural wine bar in Tbilisi), I headed off to the temple as the sun was setting. The men were downstairs, and the women's section was way above; that was familiar, but that's about where familiarity ended. There are two traditions in Judaism. The Ashkenazis, like me, are from Eastern Europe. The Jews that have more in common with Arabic culture are Sephardis. This shul was in the Sephardic tradition. I expected some differences, so I had brought my own siddur (prayer book). But there were no benchmarks for me at all. The tunes were all different. In fact, there were no tunes; it sounded cacophonous. The torahs were dressed up like dolls, provoking all sorts of tears and emotions from the women, who all blew them kisses. The Kol Nidre ceremony, which is so profoundly solemn, seemed to be more like an auction. I was totally lost. But no matter. I stayed the day, immersed in thought. I went back to the hotel to dream, to focus all of my energy into healing my brother, just in case it made a difference. I returned to shul. There was no reading of the tale of Jonah. There was no singing of the "Avinu Malkenu," where the minor sounds of the tune are so powerful that I always felt they could levitate the dead. The shofar was blown. The soul-shaking sound spoke a universal language. It entered through the scapula, down to the base of the spinal cord, reversed course, and then finally flew from the heart. As I walked back to my hotel after the final *tekiah gedolah,* I talked to the almost full moon as if it were a god. A miracle was needed.

John and Niki (the Skinny Buddha) picked me up from my hotel, and we headed to the home of Iago Bitarishvili and his wife, Marina. That was where I said I wanted to break my fast. Iago's place was the first where I had seen a qvevri being opened, and it had provided my second meal ever in Georgia. Struck by how his mother and wife prepared and laid out the food had been with so much love, their nest was where I wanted to return. And anyway, I adore his wine. Instead of challah there was to be *khachapuri.* Instead of Manischewitz there was Chinuri. The Chinuri is a golden grape, and the name means "attractive to the eye." The grape most probably originated in Iago's district, Kartli. It shows up in three different manners: it can be made in Stalin's favorite style — light, lemony, with a spritz. Or pressed quickly off the skins and with a sturdier taste, it can have some wintergreen characteristic. Made with its skins, it can have an orange blossom quality with a down pillow–like plushness. Chinuri or Manischewitz? The Chinuri won. There, under the stars with Iago and friends, the bread coming out of the *tonne* (the clay oven), drinking the wine, looking at a fresh new year, everything seemed possible.

Before the party the next day, John knew what I needed. "I want to take you to meet a good friend of mine," he said. And so we went on a little detour.

We parked the car outside a stone wall, behind which Lamara Bezhashvili lived with her mother, sheep, goats, rabbits, chickens, a spooky blue-eyed cat, snake-eating birds, and silkworms.

Near to fifty at the time, Lamara was what the fairy tales would have described as a raven-haired beauty. But more than that, she had a vivacious spirit and magnetic energy. She had managed to remain single in a culture where family was essential. She was one of the last of the silk-growing and -spinning artisans in Georgia.

In the past, Georgia was a major stop near the end on the Silk Road; it is the reason its food is laced with the perfumes and tastes of India, Morocco, Greece, and Persia. The silk growers had started their industry in the fifth century, and it had continued until relatively recently. Its demise is a tragedy, as the tight weave and luxuriousness of true Georgian silk was hard to deny. But Lamara had kept the tradition alive; not only did she hand-spin, but she also used wine — the deep-pigmented Saperavi — for one of her natural dyes. A greater love for the silkworm and its silk-making process was difficult to find.

The worm shacks had the feeling of a summer camp bunkhouse vacated by kids in the fall. But here it was the insect that had vacated, died for our pleasure, its silk stuffed in bags ready to be spun.

Lamara had assumed I wanted to see how she worked, and she demonstrated, turning her nimble thumb and forefinger into a spindle. There was a slight chill in the air as she stood with her fingers wrapped in thread when John told her, "Alice's brother is very sick."

She flinched. I was embarrassed that this kind of information was being shared with a stranger.

"What kind?" she asked, her expression darkened.

"Pancreatic," I said.

She shook her head in reaction.

"What stage?"

"Four," I said.

Lamara, as it turned out, wasn't just the last hand silk spinner on the silk route; she was also the local healer. In the way people can't resist asking me for wine advice, people couldn't stop asking Lamara for remedies. She couldn't stop offering them. She put her craft down and said to me very solemnly, "Send him to me. I'll heal him."

But looking around at the animals and the place's rusticity, I knew there was no way my brother, a Western medical man, would have believed in her powers. But I promised I would try to convince him. She gave me a little bag of tiny specks of translucent rocks, for which she could not find the English name. Alum, I believe. "Tell him to take these three times a day under his tongue. Just a tiny bit. Then three days off. Repeat the cycle for ten days. He also has to have one glass of yarrow tea three times a day. Tell him. Please. He's a doctor and he'll be skeptical, but it can't do any harm, right?"

When I got back home I did indeed tell him. "Here's a giggle," I said. "The sweet, silk-spinning medicine woman told me to tell you to go to her, and she would help cure you."

"Oh?" he asked. "With what?"

"To start, alum and yarrow. But she is a healer. I believe it."

"Send me pictures," he wrote.

I sent several.

"Very interesting," he wrote back. "With all the sheep droppings around, no wonder you get sick with raging fevers every time you're there."

It was true; sometimes I got off with one day of being under the weather, but there were a few times I hovered near 104 degrees for several days, mostly, thankfully, after I returned home. I had since learned about probiotics and brushing my teeth with Borjomi water. It helped. But I didn't care about getting sick; I cared about Andrew getting well. I knew my suggestion offended his surgical faith, but at least the thought made him laugh. But he insisted on trying the chemo that cured no one.

Months later, when I returned for that cross-country excursion and the winemaker handoff, I landed back in Tbilisi even as my brother was giving up all hope. I sat waiting for Iago on a sun-drenched Tbilisi bench. My eyes took in the city's changing landscape — how the modern, snail-like bridge that crossed the water and the fantasy mushroom building blended with the crumbling, fragile city — but my mind was with Andrew. Had he received the super-antioxidant tea I had sent him from Korea and the turmeric juice to help with the symptoms? With my legs up on my roller bag, feeling the warmth on my face, I was deep into thought when I heard my name.

"Alice," Iago called out in his gentle voice. Startled, I tried to flip the emotional gear switch and gave him a hug. He had come to fetch me. We were headed out through the city traffic to his home in Chardhaki. Iago is a lean man with hazel eyes, the kind of man who is continually texting his wife at dinner regardless of wherever he is in the world.

Iago was part of the forty-year-old gang, but he began earlier than they did, in his late twenties. Like my brother, who knew exactly what he wanted to do from the time he was a little boy playing with his microscope, Iago knew he wanted to make wine. He started to take care of the family vineyard in 1998. He was organic from the start and had the first certified vineyard in Georgia in 2003. "Back then there were no bottles and no corks; that's how bad things were in Georgia."

Iago stubbornly worked with qvevri at a time when new hopefuls were investing in wooden barrels and planting the ubiquitous varieties — the vanilla, chocolate, and strawberry of the wine world: Chardonnay, Cabernet, and Merlot. Iago also stayed loyal to making only one variety, the one from his area: Chinuri. He initially vinified it in two ways. The one with skin contact created an amber, sturdy wine. The one without skin contact created a wine of more elegance, the color of green tea. Kartli, the region in which he makes wine, was right in the middle of the country, and the question I asked was, Which way is traditional?

Iago answered: "I used to think I was the only one working in this area with prolonged skin contact — keeping the grapes fermenting on their skins for months — but my uncle confirmed that my grandfather used to make it exactly that way," he said with the pride of knowing he had somehow intuitively carried on a tradition. And so, after a few vintages, as a champion of tradition he focused on amber Chinuri.

Iago's house was modern and modest. It sat a distance from the road behind the garden and the vines. He had recently built an attachment, an enlarged winery, set behind a floor-to-ceiling picture window. Soon he would add a veritable tasting room as well. As we walked toward it, puppies barked in the distance and Hebrew tumbled out of the open dining area shaded by vines under a pergola. On the very spot where I had broken the fast, Israeli tourists noisily fussed over the lunch Iago's mother and wife had prepared.

The Jewish population of Georgia had roots back about twenty-six hundred years. But about half had emigrated — mostly to Israel in the 1970s — and Georgia is now a hot tourist destination for Israelis. The ones at Iago's were amused to meet me, a New York Jew who could *almost* speak their language. As it was a Saturday, we said "Shabbat Tova" to each other, we drank scratchy, tannic amber wine, and they raised their glasses and said, "L'chaim." They were puzzled by a white wine that was an amber color and was so incredibly different from the New World tastes of Israeli wines, but they astounded me by loving it.

While they were finishing up, Marina showed me the lace-draped living room where I was to sleep that night. Then we would take what passes for a light lunch in Georgia—six courses; for Georgia this was barely eating.

Marina, with her joyous earth-mother beauty, works in the Tbilisi zoo. With a sly smile, she left the table and returned with a bottle with Mandili brandished on its white and green label.

The idea had come to Marina and her friend Téa Melanashvili the year before, when they were working the vintage with Iago: "Girls cannot live without coffee and chatting," Marina said, "and during one of the coffee breaks my friend Téa and I discussed the possibility of making our own wine. As you know, in the Georgian society winemaking by women is not traditional and not always viewed well." But they went ahead. There she was, part of a duo who made the first commercial wine by Georgian women.

Months earlier, soon after I had broken my fast at her home, Marina and Téa got down to work. They bought some Mtsvane grapes, stomped them, and placed them into a qvevri Iago had reserved for the purpose. Six months later the wine came off the skins. They had a great mentor in Iago, but the wine had its own particular stamp—seductive, delicate, and refreshing.

I had finally sampled Marina and Téa's wine at a Georgian wine fair. They were the only women in the whole show and such a novelty that everyone was buzzing about it. "Most people took it very positively," Marina told me. "They said, 'See? Women also can make good wine.' But others, more traditional people, said that women must not be allowed to enter the wine cellar at all. Some people who were against women in winemaking were also our friends—winemakers. Now we are very happy because they have changed their minds. All of them like our wine and the idea that women like us can be good winemakers."

I saw this firsthand when attending a dinner in the countryside. It was at the house of a newish winemaker who made elegant Chinuri.

His neighbor, an older man with much knowledge of wine joined us. I, as often happens, especially outside of the urban setting, was the only woman at the table. I said hello to the older man and noticed he wouldn't look at me. He didn't respond to any of my questions or attempt to connect. This might not have been unusual in a Muslim country or one filled with Orthodox Jews, but Georgia is about 98 percent Christian. I thought perhaps I was being too sensitive and consoled myself with some of the host's excellent *lobiani* (beans).

I tried again. He was from a region about which I was very curious, Ateni. I had heard nuns there made wine at the monastery, so I thought I'd ask him about the women breaking ground in a male-dominated wine scene. He finally answered me with a touch of scorn, "I make the wine there. Women don't make wine in Georgia!"

Well, that wasn't true. Almost all women in the countryside would know how to make wine, though not commercially. However, he was about the third person who had claimed to me to be making the wines at the monastery, and I had no idea what the truth was. I relinquished any shred of politeness and told him that. I was so irked, just like when I was talking to the man who had told me that natural wine was bullshit; this man was a different generation, with a different cause, but he had the same provincial attitude.

It's not like all Georgian women sit in the shadows, but it wasn't too far back in the past that they hadn't even been allowed into a winery for fear that if they were having their monthly, they would "spoil" the wine.

Lest we think such sexism is the domain of Georgia, remember that this kind of sentiment had even persisted in supposedly less peasant cultures, like Burgundy, until around 1980.

Becky Wasserman, a dear friend and wine importer based in Burgundy, recalls a time when she needed to present a doctor's note to assure winemakers that her female clients who wished to visit their cellar were well into menopause and would therefore pose no problem for them or their cellars.

For the most part Georgia has progressed out of this level of sexism, but the nuns still serve the monks, and the wives and mothers mostly serve the guests and rarely sit at the table. Of course these traditions are fading with a newer and less peasant generation. John and Ketevan, Soliko and Nino, Iago and Marina—those couples help each other, whether it is with the chores, the kids, the cooking, the drinking, or the feasting. There will be others following in winemaking, and the women will be in force; Marina and Téa were the future.

"Time to go?" Iago was ready to leave. We were driving on the dull road west when Iago asked me, "Why do you want to go to Ateni? There's truly no wine being made there anymore," he said.

"Gela told me that if I wanted to see where vines should grow, I needed to see it for myself."

When Gela boasted that Georgia's terroir was on a par with the world's best, I hadn't known whether to trust him or if he was merely being nationalistic in sentiment. During my first visits to Georgia no one talked about the soil, just the incredible range of the grapes. I knew Georgia made delicious and unique wines, but did it have what it took to join the other great regions like Burgundy, the Rhone, the Loire, Ribeira Sacra, and Piedmont? Great terroir is where the profound geology events occur—the great volcanic eruptions, the land that was one with the ocean, the land cut up by glaciers and earthquakes, chalk, basalt, limestone, schists, irons. Did Georgia have it? This is what I longed to know.

On the way we planned to stop in Gori, Stalin's birth town, to see Bishop Andria and to learn more about his new project. The bishop had been talking about following in the steps of Alaverdi so that his would become another monastery known for natural wine. The town was an hour away from Iago's place. The climate was very different. From hot and dry it became hot and sticky. We were shown into a sitting room where German consultants and one local winemaker were talking about some sort of wine cooperative, and I had an awful feeling that everyone wanted a piece of Georgia's pie. Whether these were California wine consultants or German marketers, I feared that in the guise of helping they were trying to cash in, not realizing they would also impinge on the wine's singular authenticity. Yes, Georgian winemakers needed help, but the trick was to avoid people like the scientist from California who advocated technologically tweaked wines. The consistency such consultants were advising would be devastating to the future of Georgia's favored product of the vine.

A nun arrived with little glasses of chilled Chinuri made without skin contact. It had a touch of sparkle, Stalin-style. I wasn't sure who had made that wine, but I didn't think it had been made by the monastery. It needed some guidance, but not much. Who could give the right assistance? I felt all that was needed were instructions for keeping the qvevri healthy.

We finally left, and with us followed a small entourage, including the bishop's black SUV. We drove out of Stalin's place of birth to his favorite vineyards and the landscape morphed into foothills. Soon it was all jagged shapes and pits, not unlike the northern Rhône. All around I could see abandoned terraces with schist, limestone, and gravel. My internal terroir-o-meter was beeping as if out of control. "I used to be a contender," this region seemed to be saying to me.

The Atenuri vines had been famous long before Stalin. Even in the Middle Ages, when French monks were busy making Burgundy into what it is today, Ateni was celebrated for wine that was naturally *pétillant.* Today it grows some Goruli Mtsvane and Chinuri and the latter's red symbiotic partner, the Gamay-like Tavkveri. But it is the light and airy skin-contact-free Chinuri, ethereal with some effervescence, just like the one the nuns served, on which the region staked its reputation. When Stalin died in 1953, the local wine factory shuttered, taking the industry with it. The ghost vineyards, set up on hills that were difficult to farm but excellent for wine, were abandoned, and the village, even with signs for wine tourism that seemed to go nowhere, almost disappeared off the wine map. One side of the village was flat and full of clay and minerals. The other side was wild and rocky and savage — exactly where good wine, excellent wine, has a chance. That is where the sisters living at the seventh-century Ateni Sioni Church were waiting.

In black robes and a clerical cap, Bishop Andria climbed out of the backseat. Hiking up his robes, he led us to a little hillock across the lane from the monastery (a nunnery) to show us an old and abandoned winery that the bishop was aiming to resurrect.

From my first stop out of the car I saw we were in yet another micro-climate. I could feel the humidity disappear, the wind swoop, and the temperature drop. We scuttled down to the regal navy and gold doors of Ateni Sioni Monastery. The habited nuns shyly gathered around. They giggled and greeted. One approached the bishop, her hand to her mouth, her eyes widened. This was a beloved man, the best father, coming to see his children.

Through the doors we entered into a hushed courtyard of serenity. As a Jew, I'd never been in a convent before. I admit the air felt soothing; it was a special sanctuary. We walked to the edge of the courtyard, where in front of me were the mountain peaks, and I realized for the first time how high up we were. While the exterior indigo doors were solid, out back the church teetered, as if the whole majestic church was balanced on one point. It was as if some giant warrior had flung the church out of a slingshot and it had landed on a cliff overlooking a gorge.

We went into the private chambers, complete with expansive red Oriental rugs. The bishop and the kind-faced abbess sat as king and queen in front of us. We sat on high-backed benches dotted about in a circle. TV trays were stationed in front of each seat. We prepared to talk wine as well as ready our stomachs for the second meal since lunch — and not the last meal of the day.

I was relying on Iago for interpretation, and people were looking for me to start the conversation, so I asked the bishop if he thought qvevri wine had a future in the country.

"We need to restore this region's wine to importance," the bishop said. "We need to bring it back."

The use of the word "need" was interesting. The qvevri had gravitas. It stood for something, as wine in the country was symbolic — perhaps for Georgia itself. The knowledge might have gone missing, but the desire to reclaim it was strong.

The food came in courses. First was the *mchadi* (fried patties of cornmeal topped with strong cheese), then the *matsoni* (dense yogurt), the cherries, and the green plums. The white wine, served in lovely antiqued goblets that made me want to look at them closely—they sure looked like real crystal—was inexperienced, slightly sweet, but honest. Although 2012 was the monastery's very first vintage, it was not yet working with the qvevri. No matter who made it, that Chinuri was a very approachable wine. I was getting an idea of the kind of wine Stalin loved: it quenched the thirst. With such a pale color I thought of Stalin's drinking foolery and wondered if he could have fooled his guests into thinking he was drinking the same vodka as they were being forced to slug back, keeping clear-headed while they dribbled into inebriation. But mostly what I tasted made me agree with Gela: Georgia had some cracking terroir, and Ateni was one of the spots. "Yes, Ateni could make great wine," Iago admitted.

As we left, the bishop conferred with Iago; I couldn't follow the Georgian, but Iago was protesting. On the road back to his home, where we'd spend the evening, Iago told me what the discussion had been about. The bishop was asking for his help if the monastery needed it. "Will you help if the nuns call and ask?" I asked.

Iago had a mission. In 2011 he had made two thousand bottles. He doubled his output the next year. He was prudent, as were his wines. One step at a time. He was determined to achieve that almost unattainable ideal of becoming a full-time Georgian boutique winemaker. The only new winemakers he had time for were his wife and her friend Téa.

That night I slept on the makeshift bed in the dining room. I dreamed of a winemaking helper SWAT team composed of Ghvino Underground members. It was a lovely dream. In it Iago, Niki, John, Gela, Soliko, Kakha, and Ramaz were making the rounds, making sure the qvevri were kept clean and sanitary; using sulfur only when necessary; teaching others how to bottle; and, where the art has been lost, helping to guide wines back to greatness.

When I woke up, all was quiet. Iago's family wasn't yet up. On tiptoe, trying to make no noise, I saw I was not the only one stirring. In the kitchen Tsismari, Iago's perpetually cooking mother, stood in a floral housedress with her hands sunk into a bowl, making the typical Georgian cheese.

I made some sign language, asking her, "Teach me?" She took my hands and plunged them into the whey, motioning me to wring out the rest of the pillowy curds. Then we scooped them into a basket where they would drain and get pressed into a feta-like salty deliciousness. She spoke no English and I no Georgian. With her gentle old-soul sweetness, my brother would have loved her, and I made a mental note to use this moment as a way to entice him to come with me while there was still time. She and I relied on this connection to pass on knowledge. Then I packed, ready for the next winemaker in The Great Alice Handoff.

KHACHAPURI, IMERETI STYLE

The pizza of Italy? The panisse of southern France? The empanada of Galicia? I defy anyone who goes to Georgia to come away with no *khachapuri* habit. *Khachapuri* is the dish that everyone eats all the time in Georgia. How is it that Georgians don't weigh a gazillion pounds? It is simply supreme comfort food. Hot, gooey, cheesy deliciousness.

If you find yourself in Tbilisi, you'll see storefronts selling them or restaurants with pictures touting their regional variations. The only truly horrible version that I ever had was at the Tbilisi airport. Other than that they are either great or more great. (There was one woman in Imereti whom I viewed as a *khachapuri* machine. How much did she think we could eat? There were only four of us for this "snack" at her house, and the pans of the stuff kept on coming and coming and coming.)

Of all the variations, the round Imereti style is perhaps the most popular and the Adjarian the most decadent. There are many variations of recipes, but here's a recipe that requires a normal home oven.

1 cup yogurt
1 tablespoon oil, preferably sunflower
½ teaspoon salt
1 tablespoon butter
2 cups flour
½ teaspoon baking powder

CHEESE FILLING

2 cups fresh cheese, grated (In Georgia this means the
    mozzarella-like suluguni cheese that Iago's mother was
    showing me how to make. In fact you can use a mix of
    queso fresca and mozzarella, and if you feel like jazzing it
    up, add a bit of feta cheese for a good facsimile.)
½ stick butter
1 egg
salt

Preheat to 480°.

Mix the yogurt, oil, salt, and 1 tablespoon butter.

Mix the flour and baking powder, then stir in the yogurt mixture
little by little to form the dough into a ball.

Keep the dough in a warm place for an hour.

Mix the grated cheese, ½ stick butter, and salt in a mixing bowl
and then add the egg, mixing thoroughly. Be careful not to make this
too doughy; it should ooze. Embrace the cheese.

Knead the dough one more time before using. Leave for another
10 minutes. Divide into two balls or one large one.

Dust a round pan with flour. Place dough ball in the center and
flatten it to make a circle, dusting with flour regularly to keep the
dough from sticking to your hands. Place the cheese in the center
of the dough. Gather the edges around to make a purse, and then
flatten it with a rolling pin. Alternatively, you can stretch the dough
out on a large cutting board, transfer it to a pan, and then continue
stretching it with the rolling pin until it reaches the pan's edges. Bake
for about 15 minutes until slightly golden.

KHACHAPURI, ACHARULI STYLE

Filled with melted cheese and topped with a runny egg, this flatbread is best eaten hot — tear off the crust and dunk it in the well of cheese and egg. Make sure you have a super-hot oven; a pizza stone helps.

1 teaspoon active dry yeast
¼ teaspoon sugar
2/3 cup water
1 tablespoon olive oil, plus more for greasing
1¼ cups flour, plus more for dusting
1 teaspoon kosher salt

CHEESE FILLING

2¼ cups shredded halumi (In Georgia you'd use the local sulguni cheese, a fine substitute; you could also try mozzarella.)
1 cup crumbled feta cheese
2 eggs
4 tablespoons unsalted butter, cubed

In a bowl combine yeast, sugar, and 2/3 cup water heated to 115°; let stand until foamy, about 10 minutes. Add oil, flour, and salt; mix with a wooden spoon until a soft dough forms.

Transfer to a lightly floured surface and knead until smooth and elastic, about 4 minutes.

Transfer to a lightly greased bowl and cover loosely with plastic wrap; set in a warm place until doubled in size, about 45 minutes.

Place a pizza stone on a rack in lower third of oven. Get the oven very hot and heat it for 1 hour at 500°.

Combine cheeses in a bowl; set aside.

Punch down dough and divide in half.

On a piece of lightly floured parchment paper, roll half of dough into a 10-inch circle about ⅛-inch thick.

Spread a quarter of the cheese mixture over dough, leaving a ½-inch border.

On one side of the circle tightly roll dough about a third of the way toward the center. Repeat on the opposite side.

There should be a 2- to 3-inch space between the rolls; pinch edges of the boat together and twist to seal, making a stretched diamond or rowboat shape. Place another quarter of the cheese mixture in the middle; repeat with remaining dough and cheese.

Transfer boats to stone; bake until golden brown, 14–16 minutes.

Crack an egg into the center of each boat.

Return to oven until egg white is slightly set, 3–4 minutes. Place 2 tablespoons butter on each bread. Serve hot.

FIG. 1. Abandoned qvevri. Courtesy of Giorgi Barishivilli.

FIG. 2. From house gates in Racha to columns in churches, grapes and wine horn decorations are emblazoned on objects like these all around the country. Courtesy of the author.

FIG. 3. The roads are full of foragers showing off their seasonal finds, like these baskets full of gorgeous Caesar mushrooms. Courtesy of the author.

FIG. 4. In stark contrast to modern winemaking machinery and expensive stainless equipment, traditional winemaking tools are still in use and very effective —wooden pitchforks, slabs of cherry bark, and all manner of gourds. Courtesy of the author.

FIG. 5. A collection of gourds used as tools in winemaking. Courtesy of Giorgi Barishivilli.

FIG. 6. A peek into wine fermenting in the qvevri. Courtesy of Giorgi Barishivilli.

FIG. 7. John Wurdeman's painting of a worker punching down wine in a qvevri at the Pheasant's Tears winery. Courtesy of John Wurdeman.

FIG. 8. Ramaz Nikolade taking wine from the qvevri in June 2014. Courtesy of the author.

FIG. 9. Imeretian winemaker Archil Guriava in the kind of rustic winery typical of Georgia. Unlike many wineries in that area, his is indoors as opposed to alfresco. Courtesy of the author.

FIG. 10. Niki Antadze was successful in getting qvevri into the ground for the 2013 harvest, and this was his winery a year later. The walls will eventually be constructed with hay bales. Courtesy of the author.

FIG. 11. Didimi Maglakelidze first bottled his wine late in life, and here he is, illustrated on his label. He sells his wine to six different countries and is proud as hell of his very pretty Krakhuna. Courtesy of the author.

FIG. 12. One of the first of the natural wines to be exported out of Georgia was this Rkatsiteli from Soliko Tsaishvili and his friends, who are depicted on the label. Courtesy of the author.

FIG. 13. The night of the Chinese menu and Chinuri tasting we drank these four examples. *From left*: Soso Lotishvili's Mitra's Wine Cellar and Giorgi Revazashvili's Marani. Both are from Ateni and had no skin contact. Next, Pheasant's Tears, with one month skin contact, and Iago's Wine, with a whopping six months of skin contact. Courtesy of the author.

FIG. 14. After communism thousands of bottles of wines and spirits were abandoned and remained underneath Tbilisi's Factory No. 1 until recently. Courtesy of the author.

FIG. 15. Emzar Gachichiladze, a grape hunter in Meskheti, reaches for grapes for us to sample under his pergola full of grapes that were in danger of extinction. Note the vegetable garden below. Courtesy of the author.

FIG. 16. Niki Antadze in the arch of one of the remarkable rooms of the Vardzia Cave City, where evidence of medieval wine production still remains. Courtesy of the author.

FIG. 17. In the shadows of Vardzia stands a rare vine that is over four hundred years old. This is the White Horse Breast vine, here tangled in a tree in the middle of the peaceful forest. Courtesy of John Wurdeman.

FIG. 18. Giorgi "My nickname is Kvevri" Barishivilli stands among freshly made clay vessels. Courtesy of Giorgi Barishivilli.

FIG. 19. Giorgi's uncle in the village of Shuagora in the Imereti region offers a glass of Tsolikauri straight from the qvevri. Courtesy of Giorgi Barishivilli.

FIG. 20. Imeretian qvevri maker Zaliko stands among a sea of his vessels. Courtesy of Giorgi Barishivilli.

FIG. 21. Zaliko in his studio skillfully blends the ropes of clay into a wine vessel. Courtesy of Giorgi Barishivilli.

FIG. 22. Workers constructing a winery in 1934 in the Kakheti region of Gurjaani. The man sitting on a qvevri in the foreground is a foreman in an early wine factory. Courtesy of Giorgi Barishivilli.

CHAPTER 8

THE TALENTED EARTH

The last time I had seen Ramaz Nikoladze he was rolling a cigarette outside of a limestone cave in the Loire. Wearing a wool snood and capelet — traditional Georgian garb — he looked like a character out of *Lord of the Rings*. But as he drove up with his wife in a cloud of Kartli dust, he was all summery. He emerged from his car wearing a Mao worker-type of billed cap and a T-shirt that said "Nul n'est censé ignorer la Loire" (Do not ignore the Loire). I thought that could easily be said about Georgia.

I first met Ramaz as part of the initial natural wine gang of friends — Niki, John, Iago, Soliko — at the Qvevri Symposium. Years back, he and Soliko had started that natural wine SWAT team, hunting down nubile, home winemaking talent to convince them to bottle their wines, even if only a few cases. He is also one of the more visible partners at Ghvino Underground and often is manning the bar, commuting between Tbilisi and his vines.

We headed toward the wetter, more humid region of Imereti, once again zooming westward through the Rikoti tunnel. Some say that long stretch of halogen-lit tube was the only worthwhile project left over from the Soviets. At the other end was a dramatic transformation from the bleached and dry into the green and wet. My hair started to curl from the humidity.

I waited for the signals along the way—first the peasants selling foraged fruit, vegetables, occasionally heavenly chanterelles, and Caesar mushrooms. But this was June, the season of cherry paradise. As we pushed west we came to the town that specialized in boat-shaped flat sweet bread. Then came the potters. "So what's Archil's land like?" I asked Ramaz.

"Wait. Wait. You'll see," he said to me.

The road we took off the main highway was very much like an overgrown mountain road in California; I almost expected to see coppery madrona trees. Instead it was awash in cherry, mulberry, and pomegranate. A lank, sandy-haired man, Archil, was waiting for us with expectation.

Archil Guriava looked like a pale math student despite the fact that he worked long and hard in the sun. Wasting no time, he guided us along a pastoral lane behind his house, underneath mulberry trees with their tubular, beaded fruit hanging from their branches like tiny Christmas ornaments. This rural landscape was typical, cut up into small plots from the original Soviet rationing. It was the first of many vineyards where I'd see the multipurpose approach. I had read about old-fashioned plots, especially in southern Italy, were one small section of land was used to grow everything. In France the idea of growing corn on the same ground where vines grew was considered absurd—the conventional wisdom was that they were incompatible—but in Georgia, especially in the west, it was a thriving tradition. All of these plots were secured behind a sometimes spindly wire gate. Proudly Archil unhooked his. His vines were trellised high, close to pergola height. I started to stomp on the ground, definitely, loudly.

"What are you doing?" asked Ramaz.

"In case there are vipers," I confessed. I hadn't seen one, but from what I'd heard, there were vipers all over the vines. In the spring they mate, and if they're disturbed by chance, they cause trouble. Sometimes they're not only in the vineyard. Gela told a story about walking into his winery and having a viper, resting on the lintel, fall on his neck when he opened the door. He flicked it off quickly and then cut its head off with the wine tool in his hand.

"There aren't vipers in the west, and so there are none in Imereti," Ramaz said, as Archil looked on, wondering what we were talking about. I was relieved and went back to indulging in the beauty with peace.

The wine Archil is most known for is the meaty local red variety from the Otskhanuri Sapere vines. In June these looked like bunched plump figs — or, in vine terms, the berries hang in a loose formation as if the fruit of a wild vine. And underneath were the other vines — potatoes, tomatoes, peas, and beans. They all grew in the mustard-colored soil.

Archil knelt down, grabbed something, then opened his fist to show me a rock the color of a yellowed bone. Embedded in it were mini shells and ancient chalky crustaceans. "Ah," I said, "that's why the soil is such an ochre color." The red terra-cotta soil was mixed with the white and yellow limestone fossils. More to the point was that limestone mixed in with clay is the benchmark of all great soils. For lands such as Piedmont and Burgundy, it was a key factor in glorious wine.

Not only was the soil intoxicating, the air was too. I stood up, bent my head back, and inhaled the hills, the sounds, and the perfume. I was heady with the sensuality of it all. Knit into the insects and birds were the grapes, peaches, plums, apricots, shade, and sun — a thriving sexual frenzy of fertility. Summer was about to burst. Everything was in balance in a robust ecosystem. I thought about all the world's winemakers trying to study biodiversity; they were busy with co-planting beneficial herbs, flowers, and clovers in the vineyards. But here it was in this vineyard, with no architect trying to design it.

People talk of biodynamics; they take inspiration from that kind of homeopathic farming. They pay homage to its father, Rudolf Steiner. To hell with it, I thought. I was in a completely different thought zone, and I was heading for a rant of a very different dimension. Where I was going was Freud; farming and Freud.

Freud's *Civilization and Its Discontents* was suddenly screamingly relevant to me, especially as the father of psychotherapy counterpointed instinctual freedom with civilization's demand for conformity. What could be more illustrative of this than the theater of a vineyard? I started to see that the vine was the equivalent of a chicken longing to run free. Men exercised control over the wild grape and placed it in a pen. They took a vine's frenetic arms and tied them onto wires. They stole the vine out of its natural environment and created tools and chemicals to help the plant adapt to a new home. It's inevitable to want to tame the wild vine in this way, but it comes with a cost. Why had I never noticed before that with all of the vineyards in the world I'd visited—and I've been to beauties, lands that had been cared for by passionate people—they lacked what Georgia had? This particular vineyard seemed to embody it all. All of those in the world hard at work trying to revive soils that had been poisoned and all of those who had given lip service to biodiversity needed to visit Georgia.

In this gorgeous country a cherry tree grew next to an apricot tree, next to a mulberry tree, which lived next to a pomegranate tree, which neighbored a quince tree. The variety was boundless as was the complexity of taste, and that too came through into the grape bunches. I couldn't stop thinking that in America the bitter had been obliterated of flavor, and taste buds relied only on the monodimensional sensation of sweet. Apples are segregated, grown all together, as are the artichokes, as are the berries. If I ever dared to eat a cherry in the States again, would I be able to tolerate it, or would it seem monochromatically sweet to me? I was sure that part of my excitement about the wines of Georgia was a direct result of the diversity of plantations and tremendously varied soil and rocks. My brain was on fire.

"What's the matter?" Ramaz asked me, squinting his eyes in concern. He was rolling yet another cigarette. (So much for the pure air.)

"Nothing. Nothing all," I said. "It's all so beautiful here. Even the bees don't sting. They're so happy and content." Then I sighed, and they waited for what was next. "But I think maybe something is the matter," I said, realizing that there was a frown on my face in the middle of my wonderment. "I have a fear. Once the demand grows for your wines, when you both buy more land and expand, will this diversity be gone because you have to make farming more segregated and organized? It's the same way that I have to organize my desk by piling up papers instead of taking the risk of being buried in the mess. But with that kind of organization comes civilization, organized and segregated vineyards, acres and acres of nothing but vines. Think of the rest of the world and the miles and miles of contiguous vineyards, in Chile or in the United States, and the horrible monoculture."

At the end of my monologue I swept my hands out in front of me, as if showing off the sights. "Here's the problem that's nagging me. How can you become commercially successful and still make sure this stays so pure and in balance? How long will it be before the organization of agriculture and viticulture begin to snuff out the individuality of the flavor? Isn't it merely the natural course?" It was awful to think about it, but everything that seems to start out so idealistically quickly gets corrupted. How much is just enough of modernization?

Where's the balance? Georgia is not wealthy. There's still a great portion of the country that needs indoor plumbing and water systems. The winemakers need to be able to make more money to be able to support themselves, and they are dealing with issues I'd yet to see. It's a paradox, perhaps not unlike my own as a writer who is modestly well known yet struggles to afford health insurance.

Likewise, Georgian wines—the great ones—are in demand. Companies are importing. Drinkers are buying. Japan is super nuts over wines from this country—oranges, whites, and reds. Denmark and France are heavily into them as well. But it's not so simple. I've been around discussions when importers are looking for winemakers to bottle magnums. The guys here are forced to deal with issues few winemakers from acclaimed territory face. Can they afford the bigger bottle? Even if some of them are lucky enough to have indoor flushables, can they afford the different corks for different bottle sizes? These excellent vignerons are small (averaging two thousand bottles) and not super young—few are under age thirty-five. A fair number are way over fifty and are underfinanced. Every decision they make is weighed very carefully.

I was thinking it was a lot like plumbing. In countries where there are still many outhouses, I sometimes long for a good flush facility. But do the outhouses all collapse once the plumbing pipes go in and the sewage gets transported to a more socially acceptable place far from the living quarters? There is no answer. The idea of having to expand so much is not a goal for these small winemakers at all. But they need to survive.

Stalin's winemaker, Givi, had told a friend of mine about his take on the new qvevri gang: "Who are these guys? They make three hundred liters of wine and call themselves winemakers? Three hundred liters is what we drink at a wedding!" This was a little unkind but amusing nevertheless. Givi did come from a factory mentality, so small amounts must have seemed trivial to him. Anyway, most small winemakers make more than three hundred liters; probably one thousand bottles is the smallest amount. Iago thinks he's grown enough; his production has doubled since I first met him. He wants to make enough to feed his family, make his living full time as a winemaker, and leave a legacy for his children. Conquer the wine world? No. Ramaz is another who wants to one day grow from his two thousand bottles to two thousand cases. He wants to grow from miniscule to tiny in order to make wine his sole livelihood. Not one of the guys I hung out with wanted to dominate the world.

For the first time since I'd arrived in Georgia, I was hungry and ready to eat. We had lunch in a narrow hallway in Archil's house, with his children, parents, and wife. She was quite the cook, and both the perennial and the local were at the table. With cherries everywhere, there were tangy beets in cherry sauce. The dumplings were perfect, like pinched jellyfish, collapsing in my mouth. The vibrant preserved walnuts were nothing that I'd ever tasted. They call them *kaklis murabi*—dark, black, foreboding to look at, but inside the mouth, dazzling, like wine-poached pears with texture. Nestan, Ramaz's wife, was thrilled by them and pushed Archil's wife to explain how they are made.

"The walnut fruit must be picked before the nutshell forms inside the green husk. It's essential to do so before June 24," she answered.

There we were, smack on the solstice.

My focus switched to the animated and emotional conversation. Ramaz whispered to me, "They've started to argue about the many grapes that were lost during the Soviets."

With 525 varieties of grapes, how did the Soviets narrow the vines down to the top two and the minor eight? It was criminal. Most people — if they knew anything about Georgia — knew only about Rkatsiteli and Saperavi, the Soviets' greatest duo. In my short time in knowing Georgia I'd come to love so many other varieties that had almost died, and now they were finally being resurrected. What's more, I saw that they weren't forgotten; they lived on, like some sweet memory, like the taste of devil's food cake made from scratch or a drippingly succulent peach here in the United States. I remember an old man, in his nineties, coming up to me a few years back; he had some wine from a somewhat rare grape, Ojaleshi. All of a sudden there were crowds around us with their glasses outstretched. It was a dream. A miracle. Dry Ojaleshi lives! It had almost disappeared into the off-sweet wine in the Soviet era. But now it can be a creamy, silty dry beautifulness.

With Nestan cradling her jar of walnuts, we pressed on about another forty-five minutes to the home in which Ramaz had been brought up and where he has his vines in the field behind. There it opens up onto a huge expanse where the villagers have their little patches of vines. There, Ramaz is the only organic grower, and among his vines grow an abundance of purslane and horsetail and tons of wormwood and wild strawberries. The vines are planted close to each other on top of very black soil, so different from the red terra-cotta not far away. It is there he grows two white grapes, no rare ones yet — and no red. He told me the story of an eleven-year-old neighbor's kid. "He comes to me and says, 'I want to make wine. Will you teach me?' I told him if he wanted to make wine, he would have to be organic." He ran back to his father and said, "I am going to be a winemaker."

The kid has been helping Ramaz work in the vines ever since. That's the way it goes with Ramaz — one winemaker at a time. Even if he was only eleven, there would be new blood entering the winemaking field.

Ramaz's house, a rather large country home that surely had been grander before the Soviets marched in, had since fallen into disrepair. Ramaz's folks were not able to keep it up, and Ramaz, when he was there, was in the vines. The morning we were to leave, I woke up in a room that at one time had probably slept five people, and outside on the porch Nestan and Ramaz slept on a mattress alfresco, looking as content and as sweet as could be. I sat on the steps, listening to his mother feed the chickens, taking notes in the brilliant sun. After coffee we headed northeast to Racha-Lechkhumi. It was known as a once-important wine region and maker of one of Russia's most beloved wines, Khvanchakara. In fact, there are claims that this too was one of Stalin's favorite wines. A blend of the Aleksandrouli and Mudzhuretuli grape varieties cultivated in the Khvanchakara vineyards, it's a naturally semi-sweet wine — meaning the fermentation stops prematurely, leaving the sweet flavors of the wine intact.

The landscape of the upper Rioni River Valley kept me in a perpetual state of mouth drop. The rock. The lakes. The stone. As we climbed higher and higher into the mountains, I became more and more impressed. Iron, carbon, granite, marcasite, quartz, limestone of all colors that is crawling with ancient crustaceans, and, yes, slate, that black stone that had made extraordinary qvevri. The place seemed to be a raw nerve of terroir.

Yet the mountainous, pulse-stoppingly beautiful highland-like region was gravely underutilized and way too poor. This, Georgia's smallest wine region, with no bottle-ready winemaker currently on the market, needs a champion. We had a dual purpose for going. Ramaz wanted to find a winemaker to showcase at the wine bar who could be a beacon for the region. He wanted a champ. And I wanted to meet a man who made a certain wine I had tasted back in Tbilisi. We found his house; now we had to find the guy.

"Just up the path," said a young woman I took to be his daughter. "You'll find him there."

Engus Natmeladze was toiling between rows of corn and vines, under a cloth hat. His shirt was open and his chest was dripping in sweat. He was squeezing every bit of potential out of the land. So much was grown in that vineyard — corn, potatoes, peas, tomatoes, cucumbers. Seeing us approach, he rested his hands on the top of his hoe while standing in the sloped vineyard, a sly smile on his face. We walked through the vines, my sandaled feet sinking deep into the newly worked sandy soil. The corn was as high as my eyes, and it was even a little jungle-like. It was hot out there, and the sun was making me sleepy; I was glad when we followed Engus back down to his house, where his black-clad wife had prepared a meal in her open kitchen, right next to the winery, next to the ancient hallowed log in which grapes were stomped. She busied about the table, her beautifully lined face framed by a wrapped black scarf with a knot on top as if it were a *kinkhali*. I was riveted by her face. She looked so much like my own grandmother. Over and over again I tasted the familiar and I saw the familiar. The hominess of the food and the faces just felt as if they had been part of my lineage growing up in Brooklyn.

That's the way I had felt about Engus's wines when I had tasted them in Tbilisi at a wine fair. His red was Beaujolais-like, different from the sweet, syrupy Khvanchakara wines of the region. At the same time that I was marveling at the white, Alaverdi Monastery's Bishop Davit was tasting it as well. He remarked, "Some people might not like this wine. Some might say it's dirty. But it reminds me of my grandfather."

I think I know what he meant. That wine also reminded me of my Ukraine-born grandfather. Pop (as he was called) was intensely religious and even though quite Jewish, bore a resemblance to the Catholic bishop. Both had the beard, both the aquiline nose; both had whimsy. Pop loved to eat and drink in moderation — the feasting concept of Georgia would be alien to him, he who only ate two meals a day and whose weight never varied; when he was done, he was done. He drank every day but perhaps only a drop. But he was particular, and he also struggled to make wine in our basement. Sometimes it worked and sometimes it went to vinegar. When it did work, the smells and aromas were laced with a mustiness that reminded me of old lace brought out into the air after having been in a cedar cabinet. Born not far from Kiev in the year that the light bulb was invented, he was singular and obsessive, and he unwittingly began my wine-writing career by making me his very young drinking partner, teaching me to sniff first, no matter what. Engus's wine was the bridge for a very personal moment with the bishop.

After we ate and drank, simply but wonderfully, Ramaz asked Engus if he would consider selling them some wine for Ghvino Underground. Instead of being flattered, Engus feigned offense and insisted, "My wine is just for my friends and my family. If you want my wine, you have to come back to feast with me."

Thwarted, we slunk off to the village of Chorjo. "We need someone from Racha to represent the region," Ramaz said with determination and a touch of impatience.

We had trouble finding the path that let to Murtaz Vatsadze's home. We pulled over on the side of the road, where I noticed a gate with a very typical iron design: two *kantsi* framing a grape bunch. Ramaz left a message for Murtaz, and we waited. While sitting on the roadside waiting for him to come fetch us, I glanced up at a significant incline and what looked like very-well-cared-for vines. Before long we were standing in them. Ramaz looked at the soil and started to mutter. He saw that systemic chemicals had been used—there wasn't one weed around. Murtaz, with a broad face and premature salt and pepper hair, appeared and said it was hard to farm on the incline, and the chemicals made his life easier. There was another problem: his mother.

We entered the winery. Murtaz grabbed a spade and approached a buried qvevri. He raised the wooden lid and shoved his tool into the thick, wet clay covering that kept the qvevri sealed. As he dug—it took some time—he told us about his process.

"We ferment the red and the white wines on the skins for only one week, just how my father and grandfather did it. Then I press the wine off the skins."

The covering around the opening of the qvevri came off. At first I thought it was because of the dim lighting that the color of the rim seemed so dark. Feeling my heart beat faster, I walked over closer to get a better look. The qvevri's opening was a perfect round circle. Sure enough, its lip was a deep ebony, not terra-cotta, stunningly beautiful even though so little of it was visible. Ramaz knelt down, genuflecting, and touched it with envy and desire. The pot was silky. Made long ago by a local, it was like a Stradivarius.

"A master made this," Ramaz whispered to me. There was a signature on it. He struggled to read it and said, "Whoever made it is long dead."

This was what Giorgi Barishivilli, a.k.a. the Kvevri, had told me about—the black qvevri from Racha-Lechkhumi, the ones with Rioni

River slate sand mixed in with clay, considered the finest. Ramaz knew this, and he touched that rim as if laying a stone on a grave in homage. That was lost art, gone. We had a moment of reverence as Murtaz siphoned off some wine for us not to taste, but to drink.

Suddenly, surprise! A table appeared and was quickly laid with tidbits. Then appeared bread, cheese, tomatoes, cucumbers, and *jonjoli*. Room for more? I wasn't so sure, but there was no way to get around the situation. So enter the skinny roasted chickens, mashed green beans, cornmeal — a little light snack.

The table was bending with the weight of the food, and we tried to eat just a mere hour after our last meal, at which we had been stuffed with *lobio*. We tasted the wines, which were simple and very drinkable. Then Murtaz brought out something else. It was a deep amber and tasted rich with a perfect acid. A six-year-old wine, it felt important.

Ramaz looked perplexed. "Your wine is good. Very good. Look, why are you using chemicals in your soil?" he asked again. "Your wines would be even better without them, and the land would be healthier."

Just as Ramaz finished and Murtaz started to answer, Murtaz's mother, our chef, emerged from the house and wearily sank down on the stoop descending to the winery. With a saddened, depressed face she watched how much food was not being eaten. She was not pleased. I couldn't have guessed why until she sharply broke into the conversation. Then Ramaz whispered to me, translating, "Why does the government let the farming store sell us the chemicals if they are dangerous?"

It was back to the Tbilisi cooking school owner's notion of "Bio wine is bullshit."

Mother and cooking school owner were a generation apart, and both were ignorant, though the mother's plight made me feel some empathy. She wanted her son's wines to be sold in Tbilisi. She wanted them in Japan, in France, and in the United States. She wanted him to find success and more income. But to hitch himself to the growing natural wine crowd he would have to ditch the vineyard chemicals. Earlier in my journey, Iago had said that when they farmed for the Soviets they had been forced to use chemicals for efficiency. But the food they grew for themselves stayed pure and natural. Some in the countryside lost the commitment to nature; others—like Ramaz's family or Gela's—never did. It pained Ramaz to see a man with talent, a man with the "touch"—and one with a legendary black qvevri—who didn't understand the work in the vineyard. Unfortunately, this was one family who hadn't resisted the Soviet message, and years after the wall fell it endured. But in Georgia it is difficult to rise against one's mother, and Murtaz's mother, perhaps worn down by the tough economics of the region, clearly didn't understand. Ramaz was a hammer. After we left I felt that he might have his way and pound some missionary magic. With the help of the SWAT team of my dreams, Murtaz could emerge to be the champion Racha needed.

On the way back down to Imereti, Ramaz pulled off to the side of the road near a peaceful embankment. "There's supposed to be one of Georgia's oldest Jewish temples through the woods. Do you want to go?"

Racha once had a large and ancient Jewish population, which had arrived before the Middle Ages. We walked through nettles and brush to a clearing. Framed by the wildness was a building with some resemblance to the typical architecture of the local churches, with a modified conical dome rising out of a drum. But something about it felt different. While there was a cross on the building—dating from when it was hard to say—there was some sort of Jewish flavor about it, about the windows shaped like Moses tablets, reminding me of eastern Jewish temples I've seen. As one is supposed to pray facing east, the building had an eastern orientation. Inside was a ruin, and even though there were more crosses and religious murals, those hadn't been part of its origins. The east-facing window seemed to look directly toward Jerusalem. There was no way to know how long ago it had stopped being a Jewish house of worship; all that was left was folklore. There had been Jews there—perhaps Engus's wife, who resembled my father's mother, with her Asian eyes and large moon face; the fantasy wasn't so random at that.

We hiked back to the car and drove back down the mountain in the sunset when Nestan insisted on another detour. About 1,100 meters up we stopped at a stunning pristine body of water. It looked like a lake but it was actually the Shaori Reservoir. With the shimmering surface and wisps of moisture coming in, the pines around, and the remoteness, the air was sharp and cleansing. Nestan, with an innocent sturdiness and joy, ran into the water laughing, even though she came out shivering and with puckered skin. The fog was rolling in. All around us were huge slabs of limestone in all colors yet another kind of terroir in a land rich with it. When Gela had pronounced that the Georgian soils could rival the best anywhere, it was no bold boast; I should have known never to doubt him. It's one thing to be able to grow grapes; they can grow anywhere. But only special places in the world, joined by eccentric and ancient soils, basalt, schist, and granite — the world's minerals — placed in climates influenced by wind and sun, can grow them in a world-class way. The potential of the Georgia terroir was powerful.

BEETS WITH CHERRY SAUCE

In June the abundance of cherries turns kitchens into a frenzy, and they turn up in all sorts of inventive combinations, such as with beets. This recipe is an unusual combination that is delicious. Of course, in Georgia cornelian cherries are used. These are not as sweet as our normal cherries and a touch tarter, but terribly complex.

1 pound medium beets, scrubbed
6 tablespoons olive oil
kosher salt and freshly ground black pepper to taste
¾ cup dried tart cherries
10 tablespoons water
1 medium yellow onion, finely chopped and cooked
1 tablespoon fresh lemon juice
2 tablespoons finely chopped cilantro or dill
1 tablespoon finely chopped parsley
1 tablespoon chopped tarragon

Heat oven to 400°.

Scrub the beets but do not peel. With 3 tablespoons olive oil, salt, and pepper, place them in a baking dish and cover with foil; cook until tender, 1–1½ hours.

Simmer the cherries, salt, and pepper in the water until very soft, about 10–15 minutes. Force through a sieve, adding water along the way if needed to make a thick sauce.

When beets are cool, peel and cut into 1-inch chunks and place in a bowl. Add the cooked onion and cherry sauce, and mix in the lemon juice and chopped herbs.

CHICKEN "GIA" CHKMERULI

This is the classic Rachan chicken dish, rich and buttery. It comes from the village of Chkmeri. I've seen all sorts of versions, from the pale and anemic to the golden and fat. Here it is, tweaked by Pheasant's Tears wine bar chef Gia. Traditionally the chicken is fried and then doused in a rich sour cream sauce. Here Gia bakes the chicken in wine, and then it is finished in butter sauce.

    1 bulb garlic (that's right, a whole bulb)
    1 chicken, about 2.2 pounds, butterflied
    1 cup *adjika* (see chapter 5)
    salt and pepper to taste
    1 glass white wine—Rkatsiteli or Chinuri, with or without skin
    ½ stick butter
    1 cup milk
    cilantro or green onion to garnish

Mince the garlic and divide in two. Rub the chicken with half the garlic, *adjika*, salt, and pepper.

In a cold baking dish, pour in the wine and place the chicken in, skin side up. You're essentially baking the chicken in the wine.

Bake at 475° for 25–30 minutes or until cooked.

When cooked, place the chicken parts in a clay pot (called a *ketsi* in Georgian, made from the same material as a qvevri) or baking pan of terra-cotta if a clay pot is not available.

Meanwhile, make the sauce.

Take the chicken cooking juices, add the butter, the remaining garlic (remember this is very much about the garlic, so don't be shy), and milk, then boil. When the sauce is boiling, add the jointed chicken and continue to boil for 1 minute, then serve with the garnish.

CHAPTER 9

LESSONS OF LAMARA

As a writer with poverty always at the door, I couldn't refuse when the government of Georgia came knocking in August 2013. It wanted something from me, and it wanted it in a hurry before its budget closed for the year. The commission was for a promotional book based on my impressions of the wines and regions of their country. That's when John Wurdeman Skyped me with a big idea.

"Hey, Alice," he said. His eyes flashed. "Let's make ourselves our own little artists' colony. You'll bring your computer and notebooks. I'll bring my easel and paints. Then we'll go together to Meskheti, Guria, Adjara, regions still unknown to me. It will be great."

I was trapped in my New York City apartment in the August heat and humidity, and it sounded heavenly. Time to think. Time to create. Time. But I was running out of it on many different levels.

The closer we came to the departure date, problems started to pop up. John's harvest needed more attention. I couldn't stay as long as I would have liked. I needed to get my research done and return home. My brother was failing. As his discomfort turned to pain, I found that I, so many miles away from him, took to pacing in my apartment like a lunatic. The thought of potentially missing the last moments I could see him caused even greater panic. He had just been accepted into an experimental program in Arizona, so it wasn't like I could even see him at all. "Go. Just don't stay too long," he advised.

In the end John and I had to shrink what would have been a hearty three-week voyage into five or six days. It was not looking good for indulgent creativity. It would have to be direct to work.

I left that year immediately after breaking my fast—yes, Yom Kippur again, but this time I had spent it in New York City.

Gela Patashvili picked me up, and he had a surprise with him: Camille Lapierre, a bouncy young woman with tight blond ringlets. She had traveled from the Beaujolais to work the Pheasant's Tears harvest. Camille was the daughter of the man considered the father of France's natural wine renaissance, the late Marcel Lapierre. There it was, another example of the growing connection between the natural winemakers of France and those of Georgia.

"How's it going?" I asked Camille, who would leave in a few weeks to deal with her own harvest in the Beaujolais.

"There's nothing to do!" Camille said. "The winemaking is so simple, I'm underemployed."

When we got to Signaghi two hours later, I was impatient to get my schedule in order and get on the road again. I was weary from my flight as I waited at the Pheasant's Tears wine bar. An energetic John put a glass of wine in my hand and stated, "Camille is coming too. Is it all right?"

Camille hadn't known about this plan for her, but she certainly wasn't against it.

"Will Gela come too?" I asked.

"He can't. He has to fly to France."

"What?" I asked. I couldn't imagine what would pull Gela away from a harvest that hadn't quite finished.

At that very moment the qvevris that the craftsman Zaliko had finished were on a truck somewhere in Germany, heading their way to Paris and then to the Loire and the Beaujolais, where Thierry Puzelat and friends waited. Gela was going to help plant at least Thierry's qvevris into the ground. It was the friendly thing to do. I would have loved to witness Gela, who had no other language than Georgian, dealing with the French authorities.

"Of course I don't mind," I replied.

"And," John added, sheepishly, "I'm sorry. We can't leave in the morning."

I had so little time. I needed to make the most of every second. "So we leave in the afternoon?" I asked.

I felt the pressure of the hours when he said, "Sorry; we'll have to spend another day here. There's a visitor from California I have to take care of tomorrow."

Something about the way he said it raised my suspicions. But what the hell; I started to think that maybe I could use an extra day of not being on the road, to get focused before we went into overdrive. And as we were delayed already, I took advantage. "We have time now, so I want to see Lamara," I said.

The next morning we drove the twenty-five minutes from Signaghi to Lamara Bezhashvili's house. We passed the ever-present swinging meat carcasses on the sides of endless dusty roads, past the strolling cows and goats, until we made a right turn onto a village side street and parked in front of the high walls that protected her animal-friendly Eden.

I'd last seen Lamara when I was there with John and his family. It was then around the summer solstice; the silkworm houses had been fabulously full and frenzied. The insects, all furry and soft — they had just woken up from their final slumber cycle (they have four sleep cycles) — were as hungry as teenage boys. Pulling branches from the mulberry trees, Lamara had said to us, "No one is allowed in to visit them who doesn't bring food." She stuffed our arms with the branches, full of huge leaves, instructing us, "Take these in." A couple of worms, she said, could decimate a whole mulberry tree in a couple of days.

John's daughter and I had spoiled the creatures with their favorite delicacy. Later we sat by the an old tree stump, munching on almonds and hazelnuts from Lamara's trees and drinking the wine she had, left over from the last year's harvest.

This time, in October, all was dormant, just as it had been the first time I had walked behind the walls into her menagerie in 2012. Lamara's own wine bubbled away, and her new crop of mulberry fruit *chacha* was ready to sip. We pushed in the door to her Eden, and there she was, almost age defying. This is in part because of a bubbly childhood sense of wonder and, on top of that, sassiness — beauty and wisdom. I looked at her and thought, Now there's a woman who embodies the spirit of natural qvevri wine.

Inside her sanctuary, as we sat under the mulberry trees, there was no noise except for the singing birds. In her piccolo-like voice, Lamara told us that, according to legend, the silkworm was a special gift God gave to Job. She was attached to this craft, which had been handed down to her from her ancestors. "The worms give me so much," she said; "they know when I enter to take care of them; I can feel the change in their spirit." And, in true Georgian spirit, there's no waste to be found on a silk farm, and that includes the worm excrement.

"Oh yes," she said, focused intently on her listener as she spoke, hands waving about for emphasis. "[The excrement] is merely processed mulberry leaves, so what's so bad about that? A little sack of it under your pillow improves the eyesight, promotes brainpower, removes toxins, and cools blood heat. A little sack near your computer is all you need to intercept the harmful ion waves."

Then she asked me, "How is your brother?"

"The news is not good," I said.

Tears welled up in her eyes. There was something here that went deeper than compassion. I wasn't exactly sure why, though I assumed it was her deeply empathic nature. "I know I could have helped him. He can still come," she said as three red-winged chickens squawked by.

We moved to the shaded table, and the dishes started to come out. Lamara's cooking had an unusual delicacy in a country where food flavors are bold. Take, for example, her *jonjoli*, the perennial standby at any Georgian table. This salt-cured fermented food is addictive for me. Instead of the flowers from the bladderwort bush, Lamara used acacia tree blossoms, which impart a delicious floral quality and which, along with their medicinal properties, are thought to be an aphrodisiac. Her pile of fluffy white cornmeal topped by fresh feta-like cow cheese was very much like the *mamaliga* of my shtetl relatives. Fueled by her

Rkatsiteli, Lamara started to rattle off remedies as if she were channeling them, prefacing her list with, "Every plant in Georgia is used for something." Walnut leaves are better than nettles for treatment, yarrow leaves are remarkable, and she went on about the power of grapes for all sorts of ailments. She brought out her almost-rosé-colored wine, homemade from the past year. Then we went back to feasting, and she talked about her grandmother.

"What was the most important lesson she taught you?" I asked her, expecting to hear that it was from her grandmother that Lamara had learned her medicine.

"How to love," she answered, with no hesitation.

It was not the answer I expected. I expected her to tell me that the ancient knowledge she had came from her grandmother.

I had come to realize that when a Georgian gives love, it is full and unconditional. And, giving me another example of unconditional love, Lamara started a toast. "God made the deer, one of the most beautiful creatures, but one day a deer so weary from running away from the wolves cried out to its maker, 'If you love me so much, why did you make wolf, who is making my life miserable?' So God took the wolves away, and in time the deer stopped jumping and got fat, lazy, and ugly. And then the deer realized, 'Dear God, now I see why you made the wolf—so that I would stay sharp and lithe.' We need to drink for our enemies!"

As I left, Lamara gave me a little plastic bag filled with raw puffy silk. I was supposed to moisten it and cleanse my face with it. "Silk cotton is an antiseptic," she said, "and will keep your skin youthful." I didn't know about that. But I figured if I, like Lamara, started with love, anything could be possible. We said our good-byes and headed back to Signaghi.

After I finished packing my suitcase for our delayed road trip, which was to start in the morning, I walked out of John's house and past the town square in the still blue evening up to Pheasant's Tears. There sat the usual United Nations scene—visitors from China, Norway, and even someone from India.

John sat at a table off in the garden, in candlelight, pouring. That's when I saw the truth about the mysterious visitor from California. There, holding forth over a glass of a wine made from the Kisi grape, was the very same wine consultant who went around talking about postmodern winemaking, advising the use of heavy corrective technology. He was the very man I had warned to keep his hands and machines off of Georgian wines. He had put me up on his website's wall of shame for my own terrible crime: advocating natural wine. I laughed about that one, but there had been one time in the past year when he had gone too far. Far from laughing, I threatened a slander suit when he wrote lies about me that he was forced to withdraw when I presented the publisher with the truth. As he came toward me, I grew tense.

"Behave," John's eyes said to me.

Mr. Reverse Osmosis, as I'd come to think of him, put out his hand to me.

"Under the circumstances, I can't take that, you understand," I said. Despite my reputation of being a hard-ass, I am a full believer in peace and rarely hold grudges. But one of the lessons of growing older for me has been that, in truth, some people are trouble. I could be civil, however, as long as I made perfectly sure he knew where the difficulty lay. "Look, let's make a pact to agree to disagree and leave it at that," I said, disarming him from the fight he must have thought I'd provoke.

He didn't know what I was referring to. I clarified: "*Decanter* magazine? The fact that you purposely put words in my mouth that I never said—for what purpose I cannot and do not want to fathom?"

He murmured some sort of apology. Not feeling that the matter was resolved, I nevertheless took his hand.

"And let's not try to kill each other," I added. "Shall we?"

We didn't speak again, but after that I was better able to share the air with him.

But the Georgian wines were casting their spells. In time, Mr. Reverse Osmosis was so mellow that I wondered whether John had slipped him one of Lamara's tonics. I watched carefully as he imbibed. The wines he seemed to be enjoying that night didn't have the digital flavors he promoted back home or in Georgia. Instead they had wild layers. As I stood there observing, I wondered how one could accept these wines in situ but still feel the need to change them instead of encouraging them.

Like dishes at a *supra*, people kept on piling up, and just as I was digging into some of Chef Gia's wild creeping vine and piling on the *adjika*, two Japanese women, photographers, walked in. I had seen them many times before, mostly in France; they hung out in and around the natural winemakers there and had recently developed an obsession with Georgia. Keiko was the small and perky one, Maika, the tall and serious one. I had last seen them just a few months before. There had been an argument. Maika had felt she had to defend Keiko against a man who had insulted her petite partner. Her tactic was to dump a pitcher of Saperavi over the guy's head. As she drenched him in the blood-red wine, she screamed at him so loudly that we thought someone was going to get beheaded.

With that scene imprinted in my memory, I waved to them and then started to talk to Niki, who sat by me.

I hadn't seen Niki, the Skinny Buddha, for a while. He'd been absorbed with getting his winery built; time was pressing in on him. As I wrapped my arms around him for a hug, I realized I could feel his bones under my hands. He had been working so intensely that food had become irrelevant.

"Are the qvevri in the ground yet?" I asked.

He shook his head mournfully and said softly, "No."

"Everyone has picked," I said, worried about what he would do.

He shrugged and looked upward. I guess it was in God's hands. "You go to Meskheti tomorrow?"

"Yes!" I answered.

"I'll come too," he said.

"But harvest? And getting your winery built! Niki, are you sure?"

"It will be good. No worries," he said.

It was then that John pulled me aside and asked me if I would mind if the two Japanese women could join our adventure.

"Why not?" I answered. In my mind this was getting to be one long line of a conga dance. I wondered how many more people we were going to add on. That's the way it rolls in Georgia, whether at the *supra* or on the road; guests just keep on accumulating.

We were at least thirty people around the long table. The drinking gathered momentum. Out came the *kantsis*. I'd seen them around in all sorts of sizes, but on this occasion John brought out the mother of all horns. I was worried because once the horns come out, a hangover is lurking on the other side, even if the wine in the *kantsis* is natural. The only difference is that you can drink more of it before the hangover is achieved.

Our *tamada*, John, stood up and spoke in a night that was replete with singing and frantic dancing. Nodding toward young Camille, he said, "I am drinking for traditions and for Camille's father, Marcel, who launched a revolution by looking to the past." John drained the horn with as much conviction as Russians are known to knock back vodka.

In the spirit of *alaverdi* (passing the toast), Gela stood up to continue the theme, which was about Camille but also about those no longer with us but who had left legacies.

"The wine my grandfather made was possible because his heart was open," Gela began. "He had no confession to make and slept well at night. I'm not going to give poison to other people. Like my grandfather, I will give people something natural and wonderful. Marcel was able to give this very thing to the people. He left this life but left his children behind. Camille, we will soak up the love for your father, everything that he wanted to do, and give it back to the world. This will be your life. I want to drink first to the memory of your father, Camille, and for you to continue his vision. This is extremely important. Everything I do in the vines and in the qvevri, I ask: Will there be a child that will continue this art and way of life? Do my children see? Will they go on?"

I looked over to Mr. Reverse Osmosis to see if he was getting the message about carrying on a lineage, of having something to say, not something to sell. He was an emotional and feeling man even though we certainly spoke different languages. He understood pain.

The horn eventually landed with Ketevan, who stood up wearing a mischievous smile: "This is a horn, and I'll drink it. But it is also wine, and that is truth," she said. I wasn't quite sure what she meant, but she spoke with so much authority that I didn't doubt her for a second. Then it came to me.

I stood up and held the horn. I filled it with wine but not to its fullest, hoping no one would catch my subterfuge. And not knowing how to match the poetry around me, I became nervous. My fallback shy toast, "To Georgia," wouldn't do this time. I started, not even knowing what I would say until it came out of me: "I would like to drink to first times," I said. "Looking around me, I see the faces of people here in this country for the first time. Whether falling in love for the first time or first tasting a stunning new fruit or the first time you see a Picasso or the first time you drink a naturally made wine, there is nothing like that shock of recognition, the flood of emotion, the electricity. This is no longer the first time for me in Georgia, but I cherish each time I am here, and I cherish, as well as you will, the first moments of arrival, the first bites of a radish or a cherry, the first time there's singing at the table, the first time you drink from the horn, and the first time you recognize that, yes, this is Georgia." I drained my horn, thinking, "For my brother."

Touched by the night and the wine, Mr. Reverse Osmosis took out a guitar and started to sing about truth. The man had embraced the feelings around him. Georgia has that effect on people. I was still nervous. While the Georgian government is, to my knowledge, one of the first to fully support its natural winemakers, it is also prey to the many people who want to shape the wines to some ridiculous market ideal. This is the land of Ilia Chavchavadze, the sainted man who spearheaded the revival of the Georgian national movement in the second half of the nineteenth century and defended the honor of pure wines when he wrote, "Everything that is added into natural wine is fake. And the beverage mixed this way is not wine anymore but a fabricated drink. Let's place only true wines on the market."

I looked over at Mr. Reverse Osmosis and wondered: Is it the way of the world to steal virtue even while admiring it? This was something else Andrew and I had in common. Both whistleblowers, we feel compelled to protect virtue.

Mr. Reverse Osmosis did know pain; his wife had recently died. From his music I was sure he was a feeling man, yet that didn't mean he wasn't problematic. But I remembered the words of Lamara, and I saw that the Californian was the wolf to Georgia's deer. People like him would only make the natural winemakers in this country sharper, more determined, and better winemakers on their own terms. Like with falling in love, one has to trust one's instincts. My instinct was that in Georgia, where families live together (or at least weekend together), there is no feasting without drinking to those no longer with us; there is no feasting without remembering the country's blood-soaked soil and remembering its history and truth. Its wine legacy will be strong enough to stand up to the outside world, which will put pressure on it to modernize and change. It reminded me of something a friend of mine had once told me as I was frantically looking for a misplaced object: what is yours can never really be lost.

LAMARA'S MEDICINE

Lamara is a great cook, and though I'm not a fan of *mchadi*, hers, laced with smoked cheese, make them worth the calories. But more useful were her recipes for health. These came not from her grandmother but from years of studying ancient medical and herbal texts.

- For regularity: Purslane! Preserve it in salt, as you would the bladderwort or linden. Eat it over the winter.
- For sores: Yarrow tea or tincture, for any kind of lip or mouth sore. It cleans out the gall bladder, intestines, kidneys, gynecological parts. It is an immune system stimulator with antiseptic properties. The herb has phenomenal talent. There are thousands of uses for it.
- For vine health: Applying a tincture of walnut leaves on vines is even better than using nettles. Walnuts are very serious medicine.

- To cure obstructive sleep apnea: For a month, every time you wake, make a gagging motion fifty times, as if you're about to heave. It is like physical therapy for the muscle that is needed to keep you snore-free.
- Pancreatic cancer: It is difficult to cure, but something that certainly won't hurt is 1 teaspoon of sea buckthorn oil every morning.
- For liver function as well as metastasis of the liver: Boiled concentrated fresh grape juice.
- For irregularity: Green walnut jam made with copper sulfate.
- To cleanse the blood: Boil 20 liters of sweet grape juice down to ½ liter and drink.
- To cure a hangover: Sour yogurt soup. It's full of calcium and is also a liver antiseptic.
- Garden-variety fever: Whey from yogurt is fantastic.
- For an upset stomach: One teaspoon *chacha* and salt.
- For coughs: Dry figs. Soak them in tea for a sore throat.
- For a great diuretic: Combine 3 fig leaves, 30 mulberry leaves, 30 lilac leaves, and 3 liters of water. Boil down to ½ liter. Take 100 grams twice a day.
- For sore throat or cancer of the throat and thyroid imbalance: Gather 7–9 linden branches, never from the side of the road. Crumble the leaves, not the stems, in your hand. Take 1 tablespoon of the leaves with 200 grams of boiling water for one evening's dose. Drink 30 minutes before you eat. It is an important source of iodine.

CHAPTER 10

THE GRAPE HUNTERS

Why were we all going to Meskheti if the region had no history of making wine? That is what I asked John, the feeling of futility creeping in. What exactly was the wisdom of spending two days of our limited time traveling to the southwestern section of Georgia if there was no current wine production, even less than in Ateni?

"I didn't say that," he corrected me. "There's plenty of history. It's drenched in history. But the problem is that in the past—and I'm talking centuries back—the area was continually invaded by the Muslims and torn up, particularly by the Turks. They would come in, yank out the vines, they'd leave, and the vines would go back in. The vine was the symbol of death and resurrection. Whether there's any rebirth now, well, let's see."

Because I had grown to learn that John was usually right, I put my faith in him that every minute of this three-night venture would reveal itself to be worthy.

"Do you see them?" John asked, and I turned around to look for the Japanese women.

"Yup, they're trailing us," I said. We were about forty-five minutes from our first stop. Camille and Niki were conked out in the backseat. John and I kept bantering as we headed off to the region where they still felt the pain from the Turks' ripping out and burning vines; it was felt as deeply as if it were ten years ago, not five hundred.

"Okay, I'll stop complaining," I said, and then I saw something else miraculous was going to occur: no food in our future until dinner. Except for the thick yogurt we'd had back in Signaghi, drizzled with John's mother-in-law's powerful rose petal jam, I was practically on a diet, a merciful respite from the usual Georgian death by food.

Riding in piggyback fashion we drove through the town of Borjomi. Niki woke up.

"I need cigarettes," he said, putting his hand on John's shoulder.

We pulled over in the rain as he ran out into the once-brilliant spa town that now looked like a Wild West gold-mining town gone to seed. The town's commodity was not gold but water. It bottled Borjomi, Georgia's most famous water (the country's equivalent of the French Badoit)—salty, briny stuff, the water that created the salty-flavored sheep Stalin loved.

We rushed on to the first stop. A hard rain came down on us as we zipped past the hills, and I searched for evidence that wine had ever had significance here. There wasn't a vine in sight. Taking a dirt road, we drove into what I was told was the tiny village of Adigeni.

The six of us walked toward a brick house with iron railings. Meskheti is a region rich in iron and thought to be the birthplace of metallurgy. But the main point of interest was the house's front lawn with its low-hanging fruit from a pergola.

Emzar Gachichiladze, a boyish man in a vivid blue soccer shirt, came to greet us. He had created his own little experimental vineyard, fueled by a childhood obsession he shared with Kakha Aspinidze, who joined us as well. Those young men—grape hunters I called them—friends since they were little boys, roamed the region hunting wild vines, grafting them, and keeping them alive.

To prove his point, Emzar frenetically sliced off full bunches of several different grapevines for us to taste. As soon as we'd tasted from one, he'd enthusiastically stuff our hands with another offering of sweet grape berries. There was a nameless red one, juicy like Gamay. Some of them were familiar, like a spicy Aligoté that had come as a French foreigner to Georgia in the late 1800s. Most of the grapes had no names, culled from forsaken vines that had been hidden by the woods. One of them had an abalone-like mottled gray, iridescent hue. The flavors were so very vibrant—extreme fruit mixed with musk.

It was surprising that in Emzar's eagerness for us to taste his projects he was able to leave any fruit at all on the vines. When the rain started to finally pound, Emzar suggested we go to see his brother, Zviad, who lived only two houses away. He turned the grapes we had just sampled into wine.

We walked into Zviad's living room, where his brown-eyed daughter stared at us curiously. Who could blame her? We were a strange crowd and we were drenched: the Skinny Buddha, Niki; the blond, ringletted Camille; the Norse King, John; the pocket- and giant-sized Asian women, Keiko and Maika; and those grape hunters in soccer shirts. We found Emzar's brother in the kitchen, a sticky mess in the middle of spinning the honey from his honeycombs. Zviad washed up, and then we proceeded to tasting.

The first wine was made from a blend of honeysuckle-ish Muscat and the more earthy Goruli Mtsvane. It had some trapped gas, giving it a little prickle. It was a little sloppy in winemaking but not bad. Not bad at all. The second wine was packed with flavor. I poked Camille, "Do you recognize it?" I asked. She nodded. It is so rare that a wine tastes exactly like the grape it came from, but this case was pure and direct, iridescent fruit to wine glass. The wines weren't made in qvevri but in glass jars. The wines had so much to say and said it so well that I wrote down in my book that with a little help, a qvevri, and some mentorship, a star winemaker would be made. Zviad had talent. John noticed it too. "Did you ever think of bottling? he asked Zviad. We could use a wine from this region at Ghvino Underground."

"That would be my dream," Zviad replied with such feeling that I felt that for him it was the equivalent of my being told the novel I had had in my drawer for years was going to be published. This desire to bottle was brave because in that part of Georgia, rural and far away from commercial practices, the local bottled wine was inferior to homemade — just as in Soviet times, before the fall. Zviad wanted to be part of the future, where the bottle would be trusted.

Zviad did sell locally, even if not in bottles. With not enough grapes being grown in his area, he purchased grapes all the way from Kakheti and made the wine in his village in order to be able to sell to the village people for *supras* and weddings. "At weddings there are usually five hundred people. With 2–3 liters a person, it is a good business."

After we had tasted his sweet propolis and knocked back some requisite *chacha*, Zviad changed his plans to join us that night for feasting at Kakha's house, an hour away. He was thirsty for wine talk. But he'd have to wait.

The two grape hunters were now determined to show us every single one of their discoveries. With the light starting to turn blue, I was dubious we would get to any of them before nightfall, so in the early evening we took the slow route to dinner. Our caravan, now four cars long, pulled over to the side of the road not far from a village called Chacharaki. We crossed the road and tromped through nettles and briars, past apple and quince trees and the wild *katsvi* (sea buckthorn), to a vine that snaked up a very, very tall tree. "Two hundred and fifty years old," Kakha said, very proud of himself. He struggled to reach some of the bunches, but then we tasted and looked in reverence. It was White Horse Breast, he said. It was a grape unknown to me.

"But there's something even rarer. We'll show you."

Our caravan was off in search of one of the only vines left of Black Horse Breast, or, in Georgian, Tzkenis Zuzu. It was an ancient grape in an ancient place.

Horse Breast, whether white or black, hadn't yet made it into any of Jancis Robinson's scholarly books on grapes. It is virtually unresearchable except for by word of mouth. It was a fine eating grape, but the wine made from it? I had no idea. There was something mystical about looking at a grapevine that old but still bearing fruit.

Nichgori — the village with the cellars — was comprised of two boxy houses with the same local ornate ironwork dressing their facades. We parked on a broken road, jumped over a rustic stone wall, and started the walk up the path in the damp woods with the purpose of stalking the legendary Horse Breast. "And there's something else, too," John whispered to me and then ran ahead, giggling.

I tromped along with Niki and Camille, Keiko and Maika at the rear, their cameras emitting a constant buzzing, snapping sound. I could see that our leaders in the front knew the terrain as well as I knew the faulty steps of my lopsided apartment building—after all, they had played there as children. Just as I began to wonder whether it was worth turning an ankle on the uneven earth in the overgrown forest, there was a clearing. I could see a series of very large excavated holes in the ground. I walked over and peered down into them.

"Oh my God!" I yelled as soon as I grasped what was below me. I'd never seen anything like it. Keiko and Maika started to click away excitedly, mesmerized, because about ten feet down, with absolutely no fanfare or signage, in a rabbit warren of rooms, was a glimpse into a long-ago wine world: a twelfth-century stone crush pad. "Whoa," I thought, "the stories you could tell."

I stood above it, wondering when it had been abandoned or when it had thrived. It was history in the flesh, but its context had been lost. Surely it had been beaten, lost, and revived, but since the Ottoman invasion in the 1500s, it had been lost. Yet these people have nursed its memory for over five hundred years.

"It might as well be Pompeii," I said. "Where are the World Heritage petitions?" I asked. "This needs to be preserved; it is a jewel."

"I told you," John said, chuckling, proud of himself. True, he had tried to tell me that there was something extraordinary to see in Meskheti other than a region that had been stripped by the Turks. But talk about an undersell job! I thought that on the way to see the Horse Breast his big treat would be a sideshow of more ancient buried qvevri, which are about as common in Georgia as espresso joints in Williamsburg. How could I have imagined his big surprise was an ancient community winery operation worthy of being shipped off whole to the British Museum? How was it that this overgrown wine operation had been shrouded in anonymity, the secret of childhood friends who romped in the woods? There were no tickets, no visitors, and only a few of the obsessed who seemed to know or care. The grape hunters stood there with their hands on their hips, grinning. I felt like whipping out my iPhone and calling my best editor to pitch the story, even as I knew there was danger in letting others know. Once a place like this gets headlines, accessibility brings overexposure, and the next thing you know there's a McDonald's where we had parked the cars.

There was no time to rest or do the site justice; we had spent too much time schmoozing earlier. I never would have allowed the idling had I known there were treasures to be found in the forest. As a result, I had to breeze by this amazing place in order to pursue the rare vine that had to be seen as well.

We had to move quickly, climb and scuttle before the darkening sky rendered our eyes useless. Walking along the ridge in the last moments of sunlight, I tried to imagine how vines and vineyards on terraces had thrived, how they had once covered the landscape. By the time the Soviets arrived in the 1920s, there wasn't even a pip or a stem left for them to dispose of. The wine culture devastation of Meskheti was one that the Georgians could not blame on the Soviets.

The others—John, the other women, the grape hunters—had run ahead, but I had to slow down. I would never have forgiven myself if I didn't take the time to breathe in the place—the setting sun, the rising moon; after all, when would I be back? Niki stayed with me, protectively. We stood in silence for a while; the landscape was confusing, almost desert-like. The hills in the distance had the remnants of terraces on land so foreboding, how could anything have ever grown on it? I bent down to tie my shoelace, but as I did, I took in both black basalt stones and degraded, oxidized, and rusty basalt-based soil. I love basalt for wines. There is something about the way basalt—trapped volcanic magma pressurized by eons under the earth—nurtures a vine and brings an almost bloody taste to reds, a fine ashen quality in the finish, and firm acidity to both. "But where was the volcano?" I asked.

Niki, in his Buddhist-like wisdom, lifted a finger up and pointed to the mountain range in front of us. As the crow flew, there stood a not-quite-dormant purple volcano. I hadn't been wrong in thinking of that spot as the Pompeii of Georgia.

Piercing the falling dark and the raising song of the birds headed for sleep were shouts from below, including Keiko's Chihuahua-like, high-pitched yip of a cry. It sounded urgent. Nervous someone had broken a leg—that would have been a pretty pickle—we sprinted to catch up, scaling down rocks, sliding down mud, battling brambles. When we finally reached them, we saw the commotion. Tangled behind the wild quince and apple was not someone's leg but the last remaining Black Horse Breast vine known to man. God knows how ancient the variety was. Who knows? Perhaps it was the relative of the vine Noah had planted after the flood, a relative of the very first winemaking grape. It had snaked up a massive tree, as if racing from the Turks for its life. Kakha monkeyed up the trunk onto its limbs and shimmied down with bunches to offer us each a taste. The berries were long, shaped like slender cornelian cherries. We popped them into our mouths, the sweet, tangy flavors moistening our hunger for dinner as the jackals brought on the night.

On the dark and treacherous walk back we used phones for their flashlight function. We arrived safely and then were off to be further rewarded with dinner at Kakha's house.

The old house sat hidden, camouflaged into the hill, as so many of the homes were, so the Turkish invaders couldn't find them. We were shown into a closet-like room, long and narrow. Kakha's mother's Meskhetian cuisine was different from what I'd tasted in other parts of the country. In this region the dumplings, called *kinkhali*, were mini, almost like gnocchi, and served with garlic water. There was a hot pepper sauce similar to Sriracha and rustic bow-tie noodles doused with caramelized onions. There was bagel-like bread that immediately made me think of bagels or that Turkish bread, *simit*.

Niki and John, only in their late thirties, were the wine elders of the table to the young, enthusiastic men. Though not knowing where to start, the grape hunters were hungry for wine talk. I had feared that the only people eager to make wine traditionally, naturally, were the men and women who had lived through the country's Communist era, who had had their dreams delayed until middle age. But I saw that the youth would, and could, carry on the tradition even if they had no idea there was a natural wine movement out in the rest of the world.

They were just wanting to make ancestral and honest wine, more out of a sense of nationalistic expression, a heritage, than anything else. I pierced a dumpling and dunked it in the plum sauce, and as I heard them talk about folk knowledge in the context of vines, I got goose bumps.

"If you can't get into a qvevri, you shouldn't use it," Kakha said, even though he had yet to use one.

Out came the *chacha*, fueling the talk. Niki and John agreed that the only way to clean a qvevri well was to have one big enough to jump inside. The ones that are as tiny as a vase are not only difficult to clean, but also their smallness causes other complications. Then came the more interesting stuff—the theme of what was at hand: the nobleness of the wild-growing vinifera grape. Once the vines were tamed and cultivated, it was a different story. The issue of Freud's *Civilization and Its Discontents* came to me all over again.

Kakha regaled us with the virtues of wild vines like the ones we had seen—how they run up to the trees, have fewer diseases, and need no treatments. A common misconception, he said, is that they barely give fruit. False. In reality, as we had seen hours before, they produce plenty of grapes, and they seem to live forever. Emzar dove in to describe the ripening of all of the different kinds of grapes. He was encyclopedic. They had hopes. Bring back the vines. Replant. This was a winemaking center. Revival time! And these young ones also knew some tricks. For example, they knew that there was a particular wild apricot tree and a certain elm tree that, when grown near vines, gave them the protection of natural sulfur.

The talk of wild vines continued as long as it could, but as fascinated as we were about this kind of wild apricot and the mysteries of co-plantation, we grew tired. The journey to our next bed, just outside the medieval city of Vardzia, was an hour long. "The roads are tricky," John said. So we had one last *chacha* and headed off.

John and I were so stimulated by the conversation that I knew he'd have an easy time staying alert. "John, did you know about the wild apricot tree?"

"And the elm," he said. "Don't forget the elm."

"But did you know that they have a relationship with the vine and create a natural sulfur?" I asked.

"No," he said.

"It's amazing," piped up Camille, surprising us. We had thought she was asleep. She put her face in between the seats as she went on. "This country. There is magical natural sulfur. Gela has a problem with volatility in the wine, and he tells me to have faith, that it will all disappear. And there's Niki here, leaving his grapes when he should be harvesting because he has faith it will all work out."

"And what does it all mean to you?" I asked.

"That we in France have lost the instinct, and even if we're looking to work naturally, we need lab reports to tell us about what we should just know intuitively."

"Everyone else has lost the ancient knowledge. Others have to research and collect, but here it all still lives," I said, looking out the window, daydreaming and overtaken by sadness. The moon was full, lighting up the mountains. It looked naked and tan, just like the moon from the moon walk pictures. And there was Saturn, like a huge streetlamp, so near and so clear, I felt I must have left Earth.

In the morning there was mist, and we were officially in Queen Tamar country.

Queen Tamar was the great-granddaughter of Davit the Builder, who was considered to be the greatest and most successful Georgian ruler in history, and Tamar wasn't too far behind. Tamar was known for her beauty and gentleness, but to survive in Georgia at that time, constantly under threat in the twelfth century, one had to have a bionic backbone. It was this queen who had taken back her empire from the bloodthirsty Timor, who had ransacked the country. This queen, centuries later, was still the beloved heartbeat of Georgia.

One of the wildest descriptions of the adored queen I'd read came from a pop history website, badassoftheweek.com:

When King Giorgi III surprisingly crowned his 18-year-old daughter as the co-ruler of the Kingdom of Georgia in 1178 AD, he is said to have uttered a quote that is still famous in the country today. I'm paraphrasing, and I haven't been great about keeping up with my Medieval Georgian language skills, but it more or less said something along the lines of this: "It doesn't matter whether a lion is a male or a female—it will still use its horrific terrifying claws to murderliciously mutilate your pathetic face in front of your entire family, rip your esophagus from your bloody corpse with a face full of slavering curved fangs, and then fucking 360-degree behind-the-back tomahawk jam your disemboweled spleen into your own asshole."

This is the tale of Queen Tamar of Georgia.

While the author was having a lot of fun with this one—and I cannot find his original context except out of the medieval fantasy comic books—it does illustrate the kind of valiance, power, and steely courage needed to rule at that time, and Queen Tamar had it.

Tamar lived in one of the most spectacular cave cities on earth. As it was the Pompeii of the wine world, Vardzia was accessible, though it costs a fee to get in. It was still early enough and it wasn't overrun by tourists, so we set out up the path. In front of me were three schoolgirls singing a polyphonic tune I didn't recognize. I'd seen cave cities in Italy, but Vardzia was a crazy city, Queen Tamar's home, a metropolis carved into stone over thirteen stories high. It took more than fifty years to complete and it housed a city of over fifty thousand people. "This is really where Shota Rustaveli wrote *The Knight in the Panther's Skin*?"

"Yes," said Niki. "He was in love with Tamar."

One of the reasons Niki placed his harvest in jeopardy was to be able to come to this place, to soak in its history, to see it again. It is believed that Rustaveli's poem was a not so thinly romantic love poem to his queen and romance, indeed, ran through Vardzia. There too, knit into the cave's mysteries, were ancient qvevri remains. It was a living relic, and there was no docent telling me I couldn't touch the walls.

On the way down, another young man waited for us at the base of the city. Giorgi Natemadze had some packages to deliver to his uncle, who lived nearby.

We followed him on impossibly narrow white lanes of raw, jagged, hard limestone. Those boulder-filled roads were for a horse, not for low-hanging gas tanks. It seemed like an awfully dangerous trek just to go and visit his uncle. Miraculously we arrived with all parts intact at the tiniest of villages, peaceful and tucked away from our century; it seemed straight out of a painting on some nobleman's wall of a time long ago. Even its name was out of some fairytale: Chachkari, or gates to the distillery.

This kind of village was beyond my experience. It was hidden behind a ridiculously perilous path, and the homes were further hidden, buried into the rocks, hobbit houses hiding from the marauders. We parked and walked through a forest like one out of middle earth, rich and lush, where two young boys were picking and throwing apples at each other. We forged the creek, climbed up its lush banks past the deep crimson of the cornelian cherry, and with the gurgling of water below and the beginning of rain above, Giorgi pointed and said in a hushed voice, "There."

This was not the black, but the White Horse Breast vine. Four hundred years old, it was as thick as a redwood's trunk. The Horse Breast, like the other native Georgian varieties, were noble wine grapes, those referred to as "vitis vinifera." But here was another example of vinifera reverting back to its natural state. Its grapes had grown loose and long; it had reverted to its wild past with a sense of holiness and grace. "Ketevan told me when she was at university that this vine was known of," said John of his wife. "It is a legend. Students would make pilgrimages to see it."

That's when I realized that this was the vine Givi, Stalin's last wine-maker, had told me about. Pilgrims of the vine came here to seek its wisdom as a vine who had seen it all: pain, suffering, joy. I've always had so much reverence for our elders — the wise ones, the ones who had stories and had learned from them; those who kept the knowledge of elm and apricot trees; those, like Lamara, who held the wisdom of those who had come before her. There in front of me was the vine that had escaped to the woods and safely hidden from the Turks and the Soviets; the vine was a survivor.

"In this vine," Giorgi said, touching the huge trunk as if petting his dog, "is the story of my family." His passion came from his father, who was dreaming of popularizing Meskheti grapes and bottling the wine. "He would take me to the forest, to the vine, and tell me the role it played in our family," he said. "Honestly, I didn't feel the wine until I made my first. Now it's a passion."

Giorgi struggled to catch some bunches of fruit for us. He brought them down, and if the berries looked wild, they tasted regal. "I can harvest 250 kilos of grapes a year from this vine." He said the vine grew so tall, he couldn't ever pick them all; in fact, he had to rappel to harvest.

It started to rain once more, and we ran through the woods to Giorgi's uncle's place. We slid through the mud to a tiny cottage. Keiko, who had been relatively silent so far, screamed in the excitement of recognition when she saw the man and it registered that this was not the first time she had been there. The man was sporting a woodcutter's cap, grinning somewhat toothlessly. Keiko clutched his arm, and they led us to his little one-room dwelling; it was a dirt-floor hut smaller even than my tiny apartment's kitchen. He started to tell us some of his story. He had not lived all his life in the village; he had earned a doctorate in economics and taught in Tbilisi. But when he retired, he chose to return to this remote place and take on a monk-like existence, a path that doesn't seem unusual for people in the country. It was his past, his memory, his soul. As Giorgi said, the story of the vine was the story of his family. He needed nothing more than what he had in that Spartan tableau.

Niki said to me, "I understand this. When I build my wine cellar in Manavi, I will leave Tbilisi and live like this."

Giorgi prepared cucumbers, tomatoes, bread, and cheese and brought out the 2009 wine, a grape blend. The cork was so jammed in that no one could get it out. Then, as cool as a Williamsburg barista, Niki effortlessly opened the bottle. No wonder he wasn't worried about his own harvest.

Finally we got to taste a wine made with the ancient vine, the blend of Meskheti Saperavi and the White Horse Breast. It was perched on the edge of volatility, but it stayed there without going over: pure and with a touch of raspberry ink.

Giorgi's family was the first in the region to bottle, making it safe for the others. They had stayed natural from the beginning, but they would need to be resolute to stay that way. Someone from the Ministry of Agriculture was guiding them through the winemaking process. Giorgi said, "He said, Why make an organic wine if you can do better than that? He tried to get me to buy chemicals. He said to me, 'If you don't buy them, I won't give you advice.' Then I said, 'I won't take your advice.' Done." Not all the wolves were foreign.

There I was in *The Knight in the Panther's Skin* territory. The same unconditional love in the poem was also applied to wine. It took centuries for the vine to come back there, but return it did. If I had had doubts that the youth were not part of the journey, I was mistaken. If I had had doubts that there would not be a backbone to resist the consultants, I was wrong.

ROSE PETAL JAM

The beginning of the journey west started with yogurt and John's mother-in-law's gorgeous jam. This is a heart-stopping jam of beauty. Over breakfast I asked her for her recipe, but it will be hard to replicate unless you have access to unsprayed roses with a strong fragrance; what they use in Georgia is very much a wild rose or a Damascus rose. Remember, petals without much scent will give you a bland, tasteless jam. Try to get them just before they open. Stir into yogurt or puddings. This is crazy delicious laced into morning yogurt.

    1 pound fresh red, strongly scented rose petals
    4 pounds sugar
    9 cups water

Put the petals in a large bowl. Add 1 cup sugar and rub into the petals until they are thoroughly bruised. Cover with plastic wrap and set aside for several hours or overnight.

Prepare syrup by combining water and the remaining sugar in a large pot. Bring to a boil, and cook over medium heat for about 30 minutes, stirring often. Stir the bruised rose petals and sugar mixture into the pot of syrup. Simmer for 30 minutes more. Stir frequently, pressing against the petals now and then to extract as much flavor as possible.

Continue cooking for about 10 minutes or until jam is thick and syrupy. You can test for readiness by spooning a bit of hot jam onto a cold saucer. It should set. If it doesn't, continue cooking.

Pour the jam into prepared jars.

CRUSH PAD
IMERETI STYLE

"The grapes don't wait," Ramaz called out from his alfresco Imereti-style crush pad. Behind his parents' old home, he was working in a whir. I could see a mess of cobalt blue plastic bins, the kind olives or pickles might live in; winemaking tools; gourds affixed to long poles; a triton pitchfork fashioned out of a tree branch; and a wooden trough where grapes for his skin-contact wine could be gently crushed.

Our group inched toward him, walking carefully in the mud. Along the way, a Chagall-like mooing cow was roped to a tree, and the babbling auburn chickens seemed unfazed. We were, though. The mix of limestone with heavy clay had become ridiculously slick under the rain, transforming the earth that had been so black at the solstice into a skating rink of mud. I doubted we'd make it to his winery without a messy flop in the muck. What a vintage, I thought; perfect for Noah's Ark.

When we did reach Ramaz, he was too sticky to hug. Keiko and Maika started to photograph the scene madly. They tried to capture his frenzy as he crushed grapes in a petite wooden vertical press that was bleeding juice from its slats, reminding me of a leaky boat. He worked so swiftly, it was as if he was bailing out a boat instead of flowing the juice into the buried qvevri. This winery was protected from the elements only by a lean-to shelter, as is typical in that part of the country. Ramaz is a pro, used to working under duress. His wine is always impeccably clean, even though he is adamant against the use of sulfite additives, even in a washed-out vintage like this one. When harvested in the rain, grapes are more prone to rot, even if meticulously selected, prompting most winemakers to use the antibacterial additives.

"Alice," he said, "take this. Fresh Tsistka."

I took the cup of nubile juice from him. He took his pipe from his shorts and lit up. The pipe tobacco weaved into the sweet smell of pressed fruit, blending savory and sweet. Looking around me, I asked, "How did outdoor wineries become the tradition in Imereti?" The eastern part of the country almost always has sheltered wineries, but Imereti, more noted for its wet climate, is also known for open-air winemaking. Before he answered the question, Ramaz told a story.

The Bolsheviks claimed Ramaz's paternal grandfather's forty acres of vineyards in the early 1920s. Ramaz started his winery in 2007 on the tiny bit of land that had been left for the family. He did not bottle his wine, however, until 2010. But he first made wine as a sixteen-year-old boy, the same year his grandfather turned him on to another very important ritual for country living.

Probably some time after it became obvious that I didn't eat meat, Ramaz said to me, "And now I'm going to tell you about killing animals. Here there is a tradition for all the families in the village to kill a pig at Christmastime. Some men can kill a pig; some can't. If they can't, they must ask someone to do this job for them. My father could kill a chicken but not a pig, so we asked someone to do this for him every Christmas. One time, when I was sixteen, the man who came to kill our pig got pretty drunk at a neighbor's house and did not come to our house. I decided to kill the pig myself because I understood that men must do everything in my father's house. So I asked my grandfather, my mother's father, to help me. He lived sixty kilometers away, in the mountains of Lechkhumi. I was his first grandchild, and we had a very close and warm relationship. He liked my idea about the pig and said to me, 'Now you will become a man.' So we drank two glasses of *chacha*, and I killed my first pig with a knife. Then he taught me how to salt it."

With that vivid story as the colorful preamble, I nudged Ramaz. "So, why are the wineries alfresco in Imereti?"

"I'm always asking my father that. He thinks wine has to feel the rain," he said, looking touched by the rain himself. "I'm not sure about it though." He went on to tell me that once his production started to grow, he'd have the convenience of a real winery with water access and a mud-free environment. Tradition is one thing, but to make wine on a somewhat larger scale, even if a mere two thousand cases, Ramaz wanted something a little less rustic.

With the light fading, Ramaz would have to stop his work for the day and destickify and dry off. Selfishly I was glad; we were all—our little traveling posse—tired from the long wet day, eager to talk and drink among ourselves, and I was impatient to get to Wi-Fi so I could check in on my brother. But first we had to help John in carrying in the baskets of delectable bounty from his car.

On the way from rain-soaked Meskheti we had taken a slight detour from the main road. I was texting with Andrew and knew the time had come to get back to the States as soon as possible when John called out, "There they are!" He swerved over to the side. I followed him out to the foragers in their roadside stands. Caesar mushrooms were waiting for us in baskets filled to the brim. Though relatives of the poisonous (and hallucinogenic) *Amanita muscaria*, these gorgeously brilliant burnt orange fungi are John's obsession, and he showed no restraint. After bargaining over the price, he bought about three kilos; "Nestan will cook them up for us," he said as we loaded the treasure into the car.

We presented the mushrooms to Ramaz's wife, Nestan, and she cooed over them like one would over a newborn, whisking them off to the kitchen. Caked in mud, we left our collection of sneakers by the door so that they could be hosed off, while Niki stayed outside in the rain and took a quiet moment with a cigarette.

Waiting for Ramaz and for the evening to commence, we retired to the living room of Ramaz's parents' home. The room was a hodgepodge of leftovers from another time—Soviet-era radios and mismatched wallpaper, among other things. It reminded me of a hefty older market woman wearing plaids and stripes. Finally, as dark fell, Ramaz set his shoes by the door. He explained that he had come in from Tbilisi just for the weekend to look in on his grapes, never expecting to have to spring so quickly into action. But the sugars had spiked. They were already too high for his comfort zone. "What could I do?" he said, approaching us as Maika, Keiko, and Camille looked over some photos on an iPad. "The fruit was ready. My cousins were here. Everyone had to stop and pick in the rain, immediately."

I looked over at Niki. Was he nervous playing with us in the west when perhaps his own grapes were ready? No, he was happy, calm. He was where he wanted to be, so I thought it best to stop micromanaging.

Then Ramaz started on the difficult task: deciding what we were going to drink and assembling the bottles in a long line on the table. There were eight of us; he had arranged about ten bottles. The Georgians rarely taste. We were in for it.

Apparently noticing Niki for the first time, Ramaz asked him, almost harshly, "Don't you have to harvest?"

"Not yet," Niki said.

"And you still don't have the qvevris in the ground?"

Niki shrugged.

"You're crazy for waiting so long."

"Don't worry, Ramaz; the only thing that matters is the result."

"But, is your winery ready?" Ramaz asked in disbelief.

Niki shook his head, and Ramaz, questioning his cool dismissal, asked incredulously, "Then what are you doing here?"

"It's obvious," Niki said, with his sly smile. "I miss your wine, and you don't let me drink it unless I come here. So I came."

On cue, Ramaz grabbed his Tsistka — not the fresh juice but the wine he makes with no skin contact. The result has a lemony and angular spunk, and he started to pour it into our glasses. In just a short while he uncorked the Tsolikouri, amber colored and satisfying.

People have always put the wines of the east and west of the country in very separate categories, and not just because there is an indoor winery tradition on one side and an open-air tradition on the other. Kakheti on the east side is known for long skin contact and amber-colored strong whites. In Imereti and the west it is traditional not to make skin contact. But in reality there have been wines with skin contact in Imereti as well. There is simply not as much dogma as assumed. Ramaz makes both kinds, but his heart is more in synchrony with the skin contact, and I swear he acts disappointed if I ask for the Tsistka instead of his amber wine.

We toasted, then made more fun of Niki and his faith in the grapes. Maika was not drinking wine but was totally fixated on drinking the fresh grape juice. The bottle of Tsistka was followed by one with a strikingly amusing label; it had an illustration of an old man, Ramaz's uncle; his beautifully craggy face, framed by heavy black glasses and a checkerboard smile, beamed from the label, along with the words *I am Didimi from Dimi and this is my Krakhuna.*

Finally the food arrived, little by little, starting with the plate of raw herbs for munching and the *lobiani* bread. Once the mushrooms came out, we started in on a discussion of the elephant in the room: the lifted ban on Georgian (and Moldovan) wine importation to Russia. It set the Georgian wine scene in anxiety mode.

In 2006 the Russians had placed a ban on two of Georgia's best imports, water and wine. The Georgians mostly believe this to have been a trumped-up charge but, according to a Reuters report, "Around the time that the water and wine bans were imposed in 2006, a Russian tabloid printed full-page ads advising Russians to stay away from Georgian wine and food—a pointed play on Soviet anti-Nazi propaganda in World War II." Few believed the reason given by the chief sanitary inspector of Russia, Gennadiy Onishchenko, who claimed that among the problems with Georgian wines was the presence of heavy metals and pesticides, as well as wines with falsified alcohol. This accusation was aimed to hurt, as according to a paper written by Kym Anderson of the University of Adelaide, in 2005 wine represented about one-tenth of Georgia's exports, making it "around six times more economically important to Georgia than wine exports [were] for France, Italy and Spain." Much of the exported wine went to Russia.

But it's hard to piece together the truth about the ban. The Food and Agriculture Organization of the United Nations (FAO) reported a slightly different scenario in a July 2006 article:

"Nine out of ten of so-called Georgian wines on the international market are counterfeits. Many other countries are using well-known Georgian appellations to sell wines that are in fact not of Georgian origin," says Emmanuel Hidier of FAO's Investment Centre. "So protecting the country's appellations is an important issue."

Fakes ranged from alcoholic cocktails mixing spirits, colouring and flavours to wines bearing false appellations of origin. The small vineyard areas of some of Georgia's most popular appellations mean supply often falls short of demand, a scenario ripe for counterfeiters.

What might jump out at the wine expert here is the reference to wine appellations. Georgia has one of the oldest laws for wine production with a system that was developed in the nineteenth century. Specific geographical areas and wine styles were mandated in the appellation laws. Some of the most popular were Tibaani, the location of Pheasant's Tears, in the eastern part of the Alzani Valley. The soils were clay, loam, and limestone. Tibaani could be 100 percent Rkatsiteli but could have a small dilution of Mtsvane, and according to the register of the Georgian Intellectual Property Center, it would be "characterized with a dark amber colour, with species-specific aroma, extractability, velvet taste, and raisin tones." Other famed wines were Tsinandali, Napareuli (Saperavi), and Khvanchakara (Aleksandrouli and Mujuretuli). Under the Soviets these wines, instead of being given appellations, were simplified and given numbers, so, for example, No. 8 was Kakhetian and No. 35, Tsinandali. When the ban went into effect, the appellation system of Georgia was still commonplace on the bottle. One reason that they are less common today is that appellations are optional, and as they are more and more meaningless to the consumer, they are more meaningless to the producer.

The Russian government had meant to crush Georgia, but instead the embargo has been a blessing. The results have been dramatic. There was a drop in the sale of Georgian wines from $81.4 million in 2005 to $29.2 million in 2007. But the gain was huge. The ban freed the Georgian wine industry to go back to its roots and find other markets.

With the ban in place, the new voices committed to organic farming and natural winemaking thrived. Before the embargo was lifted in 2013, exports had almost gotten back to the high of 2005, but the big plus was that the markets were more diversified. Anderson also noted that when the embargo started, the average export price for conventional wines was only $2 a liter, but it had almost doubled, to $3.60, by 2012. John, however, observed that natural wines were selling between $7.50 and $15 ex-cellar per bottle, fully on par with their French counterparts.

There was ambivalence about selling to Russia once more. There were tensions. I was at a dinner after a large Georgian wine tasting just that past spring. It was a huge *supra*, and the room was full of feasting international journalists. In the middle of it a posse of Russian sommeliers walked in, and the room instantly chilled. They stood in the doorway; no one knew they were coming, and there were no places set for them. The Russians were not pleased and were rather loud about their displeasure. When they were guided to the outdoor seating on the porch, they loudly rebuffed the offer, saying it was far too cold. So, eager to avoid confrontation, the singers and dancers who had been performing had to move out of the room to make way for the new guests. The sommeliers then sat down and started to demand *chacha* rather than wine. It was difficult to take them seriously. If they were sommeliers there to learn about the new Georgian wines, then why would they drink *chacha* during the meal? One sommelier, with his shaved head, T-shirt, and suit jacket, reminded me of the ruthless character Ben Kingsley plays in *Sexy Beast*. As I was deeply enjoying an Okro Rkatsiteli, I kept on looking back to see if he was going to pull out a gun. After dinner there were fistfights. "That's what the Georgians are up against," I had thought to myself.

A few months after the market in Russia reopened, Georgians had to maneuver the tricky waters and make nice with a country that — as recently as 2008 — had stormed its boundaries. "Russia remains the main market; Russians know Georgian wines and hopefully remember them," said Levan Davitashvili, head of the National Wine Agency, at the time. He estimated that Georgia could export 10 million bottles of wine to Russia every year. (In the first half of 2015 Georgia sold 6.5 million bottles, down from 2014, due to the unstable political situation with Ukraine.) There are many large factories that have massive amounts of wine to sell, and Russia has a nostalgic market. It's great for Georgia to have that outlet, but even if Russia is chimerical, it's risky.

Pheasant's Tears has about 6,000 cases to sell annually. That is a boutique figure by all standards but more than a mere thimbleful. In an interview with *Voice of America*, John had said if it were up to him, he'd keep the embargo to give room for the small producer to thrive. "The danger of the Russian market's reopening is it will be an invitation to people who just want huge amounts of lesser-quality wine," John warned. He was wary of the possibility that Georgia's reputation would be sullied, as if it couldn't also make wines of quality. In the end, some fine wine shops in Russia reached out to him. "They were sincere," John said, so he made plans to deal with Russia.

But what about most of the natural guys who made too little wine and already had an international waiting list? "Never to Russia," Ramaz said.

Because of the immediate popularity of the new independent wines, there were other problems. "They're coming around looking for Krakhuna," Ramaz said in his deep voice. "The factories. They are looking for the grapes. A big wine factory came to Didimi to offer a lot of money. A lot. Didimi, seventy-something years old, told them to go fuck themselves. This is very bad," said Ramaz.

As the head of Georgian Slow Foods, Ramaz felt like the watchdog of the organic vinelands, and he sensed danger when he heard about the search for Krakhuna. Lighthearted Krakhuna had generated a fan club for its almost Muscadet liveliness. Ramaz said, "We fear that the growing need for grapes, and not just Krakhuna, will make it less appealing for people to work organically. Why should they when they could sell conventional grapes, or even inferior wine, for a lot of money to Russia?" There is still a lot of poverty in the country, and Ramaz feared that greed for easy money would pollute the desire to make quality, pure wine. Then he lowered his voice, as if the walls had the ears they had had under Soviet rule. "There is news that for the first time, containers of grape concentrate are coming in from outside of Georgia."

Making wine from concentrate is illegal in Georgia, and the additive reminds Georgians of the bad wine manufactured under Soviet rule, something from which the new Georgia wants very much to distance itself. But there are still many people in the country with that Old World mind-set: Need more wine? Just add water and concentrate, whatever it takes. They make wine for money, not like these men and women who make it for love.

Georgia has a long history with idealism and wine, going back to the 1800s. The man considered the father of modern Georgia, Ilia Chavchavadze, made wine. He was committed to the idea of naturalness, even as foreign techniques, like the wine barrel and sugar, increased in popularity. He noted: "Our people disdain very much the addition of anything but grape juice into the wine. If now and then someone, somewhere, has dared to do it, he would try hard to hide it because all of us consider it a shame and a sin to profane the sacred juice of grapes that nature has given us with additions and interferences." He was almost prescient when he wrote about preserving the good name of Georgian wine: "If it is a wish for our wine to claim its place on the Russian market and to suppress European false wines and have the way cleared [for our wine], this can only be achieved if we stand up to the European fake wines by having [people] taste our true wine."

The twelfth bottle arrived at the twelfth hour, and I could tell that if I didn't leave immediately, the roosters would be crowing and I'd have missed my window to change my plane ticket. So I left with Keiko and Maika to the strange hotel on the main road. As we approached it seemed lit up like a lantern, wrapped in crimson cellophane. Having rebooked my ticket, I slept fitfully until we left the next morning.

Our plan was to make it to Batumi while the sun was strong, so we rendezvoused with sleep-deprived John, Camille, and Niki. I was correct: more bottles had been opened after we left. They looked pretty ragged. A quick coffee and Niki was saying his good-byes. "It's time," he said about going back. "I need to make wine."

We tried to persuade him to stay. His presence is always so

comforting, even though his going was the best for him. He knew that, and we left him on the side of the road to catch one of those cheap taxis, called *marshrutkas*, that connect all of Georgia back to Tbilisi. In three hours he'd be digging holes in his land and sinking his qvevri.

Shortly after Niki left us, we passed a sign for the town of Navenavekvi. "Does that have a meaning?" I asked John.

"The place that vines used to grow," he said.

These names are haunting, like the one that means "gates to the distillery" (Chachkari), but there are no more distilleries. Or this one, Navenavekvi, "where the vines used to grow." "The village has a terroir of that red clay over limestone, like Burgundy," John said. "It was abandoned by the Soviets. Ramaz thinks this will be a spot he can plant vines and expand, and in spite of its glorious name, because the mind-set here is *still* volume over quality, he will be able to buy the land more cheaply."

"One day perhaps they'll change it a little to the place where the vines *do* grow," I said wistfully. Perhaps with growing markets the land will be reclaimed for their noble purpose.

CAESAR MUSHROOMS COOKED IN A CLAY DISH

While this recipe is not super exciting on the page, the simplicity of the mushroom and the resulting crispness make it remarkable on the palate. You'll need a terra-cotta pan. A Georgian one is nice, but you can find them in most cooking shops, perhaps from Spain. The Caesar is so delicate that the more simply you cook it, the more you can feel the texture and delicacy of the mushroom.

Remember that mushrooms cook down a great deal, so figure a pound to serve three people.

Heat the terra-cotta pan in advance, but heat it up slowly to avoid cracking. If you have a yard, heating it on the grill over coals is best, but an oven will work.

Crush Pad Imereti Style

Clean the mushrooms with a brush, and if they are very large, cut in half lengthwise. The bigger the chunks, the juicier they remain. Once the pan is hot, add the mushrooms and a touch of salt and black pepper, and drizzle a touch of olive oil or butter. Let them sit in there for exactly 5 minutes. The idea is to just barely sear them to awaken the flavor. Caesar mushrooms cannot be eaten raw, so remember there's a danger in undercooking, yet overcooking breaks their structure down too much.

CHAPTER 12

GURIAN REVIVAL AND BEING HONORED

John took off Neil Young and plugged in his wife's singing group on the CD player. In a few minutes the car was filled with the sounds of *krimanchuli*. The word itself means "twisted iron," and for sure it is the singing technique of the mountains—most notably Guria. It can hurt the ears at first and then becomes chantingly addictive. It sounds as if one song is played at two or three different speeds. The vocalizations sounded like jackals yodeling from one to another on mountaintops. We climbed higher, the songs got louder, and the landscape felt at once beachy and mountainous. Paradox was everywhere.

Thanks to the dubious wisdom of the five-year plans, Guria, with its semi-subtropical climate, became the zone for limes, the *pekhva* (a relative to the guava), and dark black tea. Even though inland the region can have killing frosts, there once had been many vines in the very village to which we were going, Dablatsikhe. When we got out of our car, Keiko was already running.

"Mevludi!" she excitedly yelled out as she ran over to a rakish older fellow with a weathered face who was standing on the porch of the winery we were approaching. Having photographed the winemakers throughout Georgia, wearing their "Georgia in My Mouth" T-shirts, Keiko and Maika knew everyone I was meeting for the first time. When the petite woman reached the man, she threw her arms around him and hugged him so fiercely that I was a little embarrassed. I didn't have to worry; the man, an agronomist from the village who had had a big hand in helping to establish the Iberieli Wine Cellar, was not fazed. "The women in this village have a hard time with me. But Japanese women? They love me," he said with a shrug that seemed to say, "Go figure."

Mevludi was not the owner of the winery. That honor belonged to a businessman named Zurab Topuridze. But as Zurab had had to take his son to Germany for a medical treatment, in his absence Mevludi, adviser and keeper of the local wisdom, would entertain us.

Chain-smoking along the way, Mevludi led us to the vines; here, too, like at Pheasant's Tears and in Meskheti, there was a library collection of grapes. But when we sat down in the room, at a rickety fold-out table in the living room, the afternoon took off. The women of the house, presumably Zurab's employees, more remarkable cooks, started to feed us while Mevludi opened up bottles. This was easy as there were only three kinds: red, white, and rosé, all made from one grape varietal, the Chkhaveri.

Mevludi started to tell us his boss Zurab's story. It was a familiar one. Seeing his father make wine, Zurab longed to produce wine himself. As soon as he had the money, he purchased land and planted vines for production, as well as for experimentation and to revive the areas that had almost lost grapes. But his focus, one on which he had bankrolled everything, was the grape his grandfather loved, the Chkhaveri.

"There used to be fifty-five kinds of red grapes here in this little village," Mevludi said as he poured the rosé. From destemmed fruit it was made almost like a red wine with one full week of skin contact. It was particularly lively, flower flecked, strong yet gentle. Once more I recalled that putrid rosé at the cooking school. Now this wine from Zurab's was a wine to show off to the school's clients and friends, I thought. But there's so little of it even in Georgia. Japan, a country obsessed with simplicity and natural wine, got its orders in for the wine first. A perfectionist Japanese importer, Mrs. Yasuko Goda, is somewhat of a modern legend, known for her ladylike demeanor, white gloves, and fear that the use of a barcode on a bottle will harm the wine inside. With the wines prepared according to her desire, Mrs.

Goda took the world's treasure trove of Zurab's wines for her country, one of the most fanatic consumers of naturally made Georgian wines.

For each new wine, even though we were drinking out of rustic glasses, Mevludi made us rinse them so that we could purely taste the new wine, an affectation that is rarely needed unless one is progressing back from dry to sweet wines.

Chain-smoking and eloquent, the weathered agronomist with the wise, worn face of a philosopher blew his cigarette smoke away from the lunch table as he said; "You can make wine only if you love it, not if what you love is the money."

Keiko, who had been in the middle of dissecting the boiled trout on her plate, stopped and then in appreciation yipped once more the man's name, "Mevludi!" Then she threw her enthusiastic arms once more around the older gentleman. She was as happy as a kid who had just been pushed on a swing. Here was a man who worked with wine out of a passion that defied money, a man with strong values, and she was deeply touched, as was I. So many small producers had been motivated by the need and desire to keep tradition alive, not by money.

Mevludi reminisced: "My grandfather, great-grandfather, everyone was involved in the vines. But now, I'm the last person of my generation still involved. The last."

Guria, linked with the region of Samegrelo, is often thought to be the region with the oldest winemaking culture in Georgia. By the eighteenth and nineteenth centuries it was positively thriving. Now it was limping. Somewhere near seventy, Mevludi had the same concerns as I had: would Georgia be able to survive? Would there be enough of the new generation to carry on, motivated by what had motivated Georgia through the years, a deep connection to the vine?

"What can be done so that you aren't the last?" I asked. "Is anyone interested now that Zurab has made such a success?"

As village elder, Mevludi took his role as mentor seriously. "We're hiring young boys in the village, hoping they'll love it too. Vines are not potatoes; it is not chucking seeds in the ground and harvesting the next year," he said, referring to the nobility of the grapevine. He was determined. And it wasn't idle talk. He would do what he could to help the youth develop a love for wine and carry on the tradition. "Vine work is manual labor. The type of person attracted to the vine is not someone attracted to quick money. The trouble now is that there's still so much poverty, so we hire between five and ten people and try to pay them a little more than other places would. Here's the plan: pay fair wages, instill an interest in the hopes the worker becomes passionate."

"One can hope," I said, thinking about Iago's experience: kids more interested in playing checkers and drinking coffee than earning money to clean his qvevri. I tend to be pessimistic, but perhaps there was hope.

Mevludi, with his empty plate, seemed to subsist on smoke and reminiscence. "In Soviet times, everything was quantity-driven. No one was looking at quality or natural production, just how you could have more, more, and more."

It was then that everything crystallized for me: communism under the Russians and modern-day capitalism were twins separated at birth. Neither fostered or celebrated the individual. The large factory was favored over the quality-oriented artisan. Modern economy meant outsourcing offshore for cheaper labor. Even the Georgians went sniffing in the wrong places and taking the wrong advice, like, for instance, from the British wine adviser they had hired who had always been outspoken against natural wine and in favor of "consistency," as if wine were something straight off the conveyor belt.

Just as when I had discovered the Pompeii of wine, as well as Archil's paradise of biodiversity, this revelation raised goose bumps. Sitting there in that living room, with the best tomatoes I'd had to date (and the bar for tomatoes in Georgia is very high), with Zurab's lively wine in my glass and a spectacular plum sauce called *tkemali* on my plate (so garlicky that I knew it would kill not only a vampire, but also my palate), I knew why Keiko and Maika had come back repeatedly, often without an interpreter even though they spoke no Georgian. I understood why a shipment of qvevri was sitting in customs in Paris waiting to be planted at top wineries in the Loire and Beaujolais. I knew why I couldn't get Georgia off my mind.

Georgia is still a country where possibility is extant. The country, with all of its quirks, had come to me at the moment I'd wondered if I was bored, jaded with wine. As a friend had said after my two books, *The Battle for Wine and Love* and *Naked Wine*, were published, perhaps my work was done. I'd sounded the alarm about wine falsification more loudly than anyone else at the time, and the wine world was a changed place because of it. I had earned my obituary. An old leftie who had been too young at the time of the hippies but who's heart was into whistle-blowing and activism, I wondered what my next cause would be.

That was another quality my brother and I had in common. Even at the hospital when he was head of a cath lab, he was willing to risk lawsuits by outing a colleague who was falsifying papers. He would not suffer through the dishonest or irresponsible, even if it reflected poorly on him as the squealer. Saving lives and honesty mattered the most. He had become a doctor out of passion for medicine, not for the dollar. Perhaps the reason I so dearly wanted him to experience Georgia was to show him how our worlds connected in adulthood and how that spirit of idealism still thrived in the country by the Black Sea.

When Georgia appeared to me, I saw a subset of winemakers who had the power to drive a whole country to greatness. The fire had been lit under the wines made naturally, the thirst for them was unquenchable, and there weren't enough great wines to satisfy the demand. And here, hiding in plain sight, were these winemakers in Georgia who didn't have to revert to the way of their grandfathers; they had made wine in the manner of their ancestors all along. There were consultants trying to push them into consistency and reduce the supposed flaws, all in the good name of helping them make a living—but at the sacrifice of their history. I heard none of the nonsense espoused by growers in Europe or in California, who said, "I'm organic—except for Roundup." Roundup is the brand name for the notorious and controversial weed killer glycophosphate.

But these Georgian farmers knew the reality; once chemicals like glycophosphate were involved, you had no right to use the word "organic" to describe your land.

These were men and women who had so much to tell the world, and all they needed was a platform. I was energized. This was something I could do. I couldn't change the world, I couldn't stop ISIS or promote world peace, but I could write about this tiny, rare wine culture.

Yet I'm not one for hero worship. I'm forever finding my own clay feet as a way to protect myself against profound disappointment. Georgia still has some remnants of the Soviet Union; there is politicizing and favors; there are even some people trying to take advantage of the natural craze who are passing themselves off as traditional and organic when they're not. So I'm not saying the country is perfection, filled with only individuals who would fight to the death for the vine in which they believe. But without oversentimentalizing, I can say that Georgia is a country where ideals are strong, where they still mean something, where making wine is the pursuit of a dream and not just a money-making scheme. It is because jumping into the qvevri and scrubbing them, menial and back-breaking work, is as noble as tending to the vines, where the wines are still priced not to gouge but to serve.

I came back to the facts: the Georgian heroic poem is one devoted to friendship. From *The Knight in the Panther's Skin* comes this quote: "Spending on feasting and wine is better than hoarding our substance. That which we give makes us richer; that which is hoarded is lost."

Seven centuries later, Ilia Chavchavadze, the heroic founder of the new Georgia, wrote the following in his book, *How to Make Wine the Georgian Way*: "Therefore the only thing left to do is not betray the true wine making; keep those Chaptalisations, Gallisations and other 'ations' far from us and outside our country, as well as inside; let's place only true wines at the market."

These sentiments are still embedded in the collective consciousness of the Georgians, who continue to live by values that resonated with us at Mevludi's table. It is no wonder that winemakers keep making pilgrimages here and that others, like me, are attracted to Georgia's beauty and come here for inspiration.

Curious about how deeply the ideas of Chavchavadze are embedded in the culture, I asked Mevludi, "Did you ever work chemically in this village? Was there any tradition of working as you do, naturally?"

"For the state we had to work with chemicals, but we kept natural viticulture alive in our little plots and yards. We practiced it with the wines we wanted to drink ourselves. But because everything was government-owned, some people lost the connection. It's true. But now, the interest is in natural, and the quality is high."

"What about the qvevri?" I asked him, thinking about that wine expert from the cooking school. "There's huge interest outside of Georgia, but what about inside this country?

He turned more pensive and lit up another cigarette. "To take care of a qvevri is a lot of hard work. Many people have started to use plastic barrels just because they are easy to clean and it takes less time. But, yes, people are starting to love the variety of grapes and qvevri wines. But these wines are more expensive."

"Is there resistance to their price?" I asked.

"Thirty percent of the population can afford them, but that's probably enough."

That is fine when you think that people are drinking less, but better, wine. But when you consider that for a wedding or party the Georgians allot three liters of wine per person — over three bottles of wine per man and just a little less per woman — there needs to be wine available at a low price. Those are never the wines that will be the ambassadors for the region; those won't ever be the wines that draw travelers to Georgia. And the best wines of the country are still far cheaper than those made like them in other countries.

I sat back and looked at the foods piled high on the table, the same foods as in other parts of the country but with a western, spicier difference. We had dined beautifully. Stuffed with food and thoughts, we got into the car. John asked me, "Do you want to see the other qvevri maker, the one who made Zurab's?" It sounded like a great idea to me, especially as it was only thirty minutes away and on the way to Batumi. But if I had imagined a quick, New York City–like stop-in-and-say-hi, I was deluded and hadn't learned anything about hospitality during my time in the country.

Genno Chakhidze lived in the village of Atsana. The town, encircled by mountains, seemed relatively prosperous as there are clusters of houses and even sidewalks, things rarely seen unless they're in a veritable city or a rehabbed tourist town like Signaghi. At one time the village had supported a ridiculous number of qvevri makers: ninety. It was known for its special clay, which was obvious from the slippery journey to Genno's front door across a patch of land perhaps even more of a skating rink than Ramaz's.

A slight man with a full head of dark hair and one who rarely smiled, Genno was not far removed from Mevludi's generation. "Our family has been making qvevri for three hundred years," he said. "All the masters are dead. I'm the last one. But I am the best there is in Georgia."

I wasn't surprised that he claimed to be the best because the other qvevri maker, Zaliko in Imereti, had thumped his chest and also said he was the best. Genno, like Zaliko, built the qvevri one snake of clay at a time. The renaissance in qvevri making hadn't hit this town yet. Where Zaliko was backed up for a few years with qvevri orders, Genno was still mostly making bread ovens and clay roof tiles in his workshop.

Just as one makes choices in making wines, one can make choices in how to fire a qvevri. Both Zaliko and Genno fire from below. Zaliko's fire is directly below the layer of qvevri, and he lays down long logs one to two feet underneath the floor of the kiln. Genno, on the other hand, dedicates a whole floor for firing, and he lays the logs about five feet deep, punching holes in the floor that allow the heat to rise. Genno doesn't have the ability to build as large a vessel as Zaliko. His vessels are more petite, more decorative; the rope layers are rib-like, much like the traditional stone buildings in eastern Georgia. Genno said, "Yes, they are pretty. They are more ornate." But he added proudly, "Their purpose is not looks, however; it's strength."

That was it. I was ready to go. Really ready. We hadn't been traveling that long, but it had been wet and uncomfortable, and all of that eating and driving was tiring. I was covered in mud and needed a serious walk to think and work off the food I'd eaten at lunch. I was at the point in my journey when all I wanted, along with a shower and some alone time, was to see the architecture and snoop around the modern city of Batumi, letting all I had seen and listened to in a compressed time sink in. So I had hoped for a miracle, a short visit. Even though Genno asked us to come in out of the rain into his home, my hopes were raised when I couldn't smell any food being prepared.

I should have known better.

His wife said hello and then disappeared into the kitchen, where I saw her start to pat the dough for the *khachapuri*. We had not made any appointment beforehand. We had given them no indication that they should go shopping for a feast. I still held out hope. But then I heard frying and saw her lay in black catfish. I felt trapped. It was not looking good for a quick getaway. We sat down. A pitcher of wine came out, along with a plate of cucumbers. The glasses were set down.

"Zurab made a fairy tale happen in his village," Genno said about the wine resurrection, clearly adoring Mevludi's boss and his best customer. He added proudly, "He loves to come here, you know. I think it's because he loves my wine."

Then Genno offered us the wine he claimed Zurab loved, made from the vine that his father had planted. It was a grape he said was referred to as "Noah's." For twenty years the vine didn't give any fruit, and Genno and his brother wanted to cut it down. But the fact that it was a link to their father prevented them, and they kept it alive. That vine, whatever it really is, gives a half-ton in each vintage. With that wine now in our glasses, Genno raised his and said, "I want to drink to my guests."

We lifted glasses. I sipped. The wine was rustic, and that is the best thing I could say about it because it was not truly enjoyable. Then the real torture began slowly. One dish came out, then another. One wine and then another. One toast, then another. Every time I took a sip, the glass was refilled. I stopped drinking. This did not escape Genno's attention, and I could see his watchful eye on my glass's level.

There were breads, there were vegetables, there were cheeses, there was that fried fish; there was chicken and some boiled meat and odd, anemically colored hot dog–like sausage that made me gleeful that I was a vegetarian, but still there was much on the table suitable for me and I couldn't offend my host. That's when I remembered that John told me the secret: take food on the plate, and leave it there. The gesture was good enough.

Genno complained about my lack of appetite. "Maybe you're not eating the cheese because you think it comes from the store?" He was offended. "We have three cows; each gives a different kind of milk and flavor."

The cheeses were indeed remarkable, but not being a cow myself, my stomach had its limits.

There was enough on my untouched plate to feed an entire family. We tried to demur. We had a long ride ahead of us. Genno was not to be deterred when another round of hot *khachapuri* arrived. "We need to bless you before you go on your journey so that it's a good road."

It's difficult in Kakheti to take leave of your host, but in comparison to the other regions of the country, it is the most reasonable. There the host must ask the guests three times to stay. If on the third time the guests remain firm, then the host can (and must) release them. In Racha it's tough too. But from my short time in Guria, I knew that we were sunk. We all needed to be honored. Genno drank to John and the good he did for wine. He drank to John for bringing us to him. He drank to Camille and her unborn children. He drank to Keiko's and Maika's unborn children and mine as well, even though that door for the three of us had closed a while back. When it finally seemed that he was done and we tried to stand up from the table, Genno thundered, "You will sit and be honored!" I feared he'd bring out a sword to make his point. He shot a look at John, who shrugged with a twinkle in his eye, as if to say, "What can I do? I have a wife and children and a winery. I don't want to lose my life." We sat right back down, and I thought of a local proverb: "The guest is the host's donkey. He [the host] can tie him up wherever he likes."

TKEMALI

Another staple of the table is *tkemali*, which to me seems like a Georgian version of Indian tamarind sauce. The one we had at Zurab's was about the best I had had, and you sample it at every table you feast or eat at. The sauce is always on the Georgian table and adds zip and tang to any food, from potatoes to *kinkhali* to fried fish. I'd even dip my *khachapuri* in it. Unless you have a source for sour plums or a local wild plum tree, you'll have to add acidity with extra lemon juice. The Georgian feast recipe calls for Santa Anna plums. Anya Von Bremzen, in her *Please to the Table*, uses prune plums.

> 4 pounds plums
> 4 heads garlic, chopped fine
> 1/2 cup fresh coriander, finely chopped
> 1 teaspoon finely chopped mint
> 1 teaspoon chopped dill
> 1 teaspoon ground coriander
> 1 teaspoon ground fennel seed
> 1 teaspoon red pepper
> 2 1/2 teaspoons salt

Cut plums in half.

Place the plums in a medium saucepan and add water to cover. Simmer until the plums are soft, about 10 minutes, depending on their size. Drain. When cool, skin and pit. Discard pits and skins. Pass the plums through a sieve. Return them to the saucepan. Reserve the water.

Add the garlic and coriander.

Add salt and cook on medium temperature. If too sour, add some sugar to taste.

At the end, add the coriander, mint, and remaining spices. Add in the reserved water to achieve desired thickness. The mixture should be stirred well and cooked lightly.

CHAPTER 13

POLYPHONY AND
THE FUTURE

"So it's my last day and we're going to a place that is so divested of wine that there's not even a vine hiding in the trees?"

"That's almost right," John said.

I had had a similarly disgruntled reaction to going to Meskheti a mere two days before — it seemed a decade ago. But John had redeemed himself. Those grape hunters had restored my faith in a regional revival. Still, I suggested, "Maybe we should just get on the road? We have a six-hour ride ahead of us to get to Iago's for dinner." I was calculating that if we left early, we could pick up some more Caesar mushrooms from the Imereti stands that we had to pass on the way back. But John had promised his friend Stefan Diasamidze, whom he called "the shepherd," that we were coming. "Stefan's mother has been cooking for days," he said. "There is no way we can disappoint her."

So I swallowed my own disappointment and watched the hills grow into mountains. We shared our road with roaming cows, pigs, and sheep, and the fields were dotted with haystacks made by pitchforks, not by machines, looking like Brueghel paintings. At one time this area was crawling with vines; were some of the old varieties in need of resurrection? Not exactly recognizable at all anymore but safely growing in some vine libraries were Brola, Khopaturi, Klarjuli, Mekrenchkhi, Burdzghala, Kviristava, Shvashura, Jineshi, Satsuri, and Batomura.

We arrived in rural, hilly Qvashta and drove past high corn until we stopped in front of a house with a very active farm with soil the color of copper. The family made everything there; even the wheat was milled on location. John's young friend Stefan came to greet us. We were making a long detour just for lunch with his mother, father, wife, and new baby.

We had left Keiko and Maika back in Batumi, so now, a smaller group, we were ushered into a small, sun-filled living room, and we took our chairs at a table that was done up fancily, with folded napkins in the glasses—a flourish I'd not seen in a home. Out came the conversation and food. John was right: Stefan's mother was a great cook. Turkish influences were obvious, and she had thoughtfully made her grape leaves meat-free out of respect for the vegetarians among us. As we ate lunch, the television stayed on, displaying an endless looped tape of Stefan's marriage, which had put a stop to his shepherding. Now that he was a family man, he needed to be home, taking care of his family. He wanted a more grounded way of life. But to John he'll always be "the shepherd."

Stefan had supplied us with his own bottle of Pheasant's Tears wine, left over from John's previous visit, but then John said, "Stefan's own wine is excellent."

"You make wine?" I said, eager to taste it.

Stefan blushed. He started to deny it. But then his shy desire for a life as a winemaker started to come through. He admitted he wanted to bring back wine culture into the area.

Sneaky John; he always had a reason for what he was doing. He knew my reason for traveling through Georgia was to learn as much as I could about the past and present wine situation in the country, but also to know how valid my suspicion was that the man in the cooking school and his ilk—the new and the modern and the young—were ready to throw Georgian traditional wines under the bus. He knew I had my concerns that those of the new generation would want cushy wine jobs with big paychecks and wouldn't want to get their hands dirty. With the bulk of the natural guys being older, who would continue along the path? Yes, there were exceptions, like a man who looked like a fourteen-year-old, Temuri Dakishvili of Teleda in Kakheti. He was a second-generation professional winemaker who flirted with the concept of natural more than his father did. There was Alex, the kid from Tuxedo Park, New York, with Georgian roots who had just entered the fold as well. There were those grape hunters we met in Meskheti.

Stefan's story was very different. Even though his family had been apostates centuries back, he was born a Muslim. Yet he had recently converted back to Georgian Orthodoxy. He had had no previous connection to wine but was coming to it now with a newly discovered passion, as a connection to the ancestors who had been forced to convert under the Turks.

There in front of me was a young man not yet thirty who would not be afraid of the hard work, who would not be afraid to clean a qvevri, who was committed to organic out of an innate respect of nature, and, what's more, who was wise enough to know he had to start slowly. He was a little timid, free of ego, but full of desire. He wanted to make a living doing what he loved, and I had a sense he would be a careful and heartfelt winemaker. Working as a shepherd, watching nature and living with it, would serve as excellent training.

We should have started on our way, but we were mesmerized. We were hooked in by the story, by the food. And, to make it harder for us to go, Stefan's father pulled out a goatskin, off of which he had chopped the feet and turned into a rustic bagpipe. Being an old folkie, I had been around pipes of all kinds before, but this was the first one where the instrument was a recently killed animal. The father started to blow out multivoiced polyphonic music with it. The oldest form of polyphony — textural music that goes in a million directions — is supposedly from Georgia. Like tarragon, not everyone loves it. But give it some time and the music haunts. Polyphony, the traditional music of Georgia, whether in instrumentation or in singing, had been on my mind since the conversation John and I had had the previous night in front of the Black Sea waves slapping against the rocky beach.

We had arrived in Batumi minutes before dusk. With the sea to our right, we dropped down into the Dubaiesque city, catching the last glimpses of lush tropical greens and brilliant-beaked flowers and a statue of Medea holding a fleece. Batumi was the ancient kingdom of Colchis, the very city Jason had come to claim in order to reclaim his place on the throne. However, in order to succeed he had to go through a series of impossible tasks, which he was able to accomplish only because of the love, help, and sorcery of the complicated Medea. Perhaps if what Jason had actually been looking for was good qvevri wine, he would have found it then. Centuries later? No. In 1723 Batumi became part of the Ottoman Empire, and the mass conversions and ripping out of the vines commenced. Polyphony endured; the vine did not.

Camille, John, and I went out into the night, to find some Ajarian *khachapuri*. But afterward, around midnight, I said, "I haven't come this far not to feel the Black Sea, have I?"

It had been on all of our minds. Camille, a surfer, wanted to not only get her foot in it as I did. She wanted to plunge. Overcome with youthful desire and the need for exercise, Camille stepped out of her clothes on the rocky beach and flung herself into the sea's dark soup, threading in and out of it like a blond seal. As John and I kept a watchful eye on her, he brought up music again.

"Natural wine and polyphony were separated at birth," he said.

I had heard the theory before. I was weary of it. "John, I understand it's your metaphor; music was the reason you came to Georgia, but it's just not mine."

"Hear me out," he pleaded.

"Even the California wine consultant uses it as an analogy."

"Are you ready to stop and listen to me?" he asked.

"I mean, it's almost cliché to talk about natural wine as an old 78 rpm record counterpointed by the modern and digital," I said. "Krug calls wine a symphony; God knows what the consultant does; another guy does wine and music pairings. Other people have compared natural wine to dystonic jazz."

He put his hand on my shoulder for emphasis that I should just shut up. "Okay," I said, opening up my mind and heart. I looked out across the night sea as the wind picked up.

I stood still.

We turned to watch Camille swim, and he started: "This isn't about digital or dissonant jazz at all. Ready?"

I took a breath and shook my head affirmatively. "Ready."

"Okay then. When you have pure fifths, you get ringing, goose-pimply, hair-raising harmonies," he said. "For the modern ear, used to the standardized, this can be too edgy, although in the seeming dissonance is actually pure harmony. Same with many natural wines. The very thing that gives them that edge is that they are not sandpapered, not shellacked."

"Yes, this is the digitized theory," I said. I was being difficult, but I was tired of hearing the same arguments time and again.

He continued smiling, and went on. "Our wines still have that glorious roughness around the edges that is their life, their purity. Their authenticity."

I felt sheepish for having been so dismissive.

"Keto says her songs might be beautiful because they are the accumulative voice of thousands of her ancestors." It was then that something started to register with me and that his take on the collective history began to move me. "Gela will say his wine is special because of the layers of time and wisdom. Keto and Gela both see themselves as fostering something, nurturing something much greater than themselves."

Both music and wine—especially natural wine—were visceral. It was exactly as John said, especially when I clocked the reactions people had to the natural wines of Georgia, reactions that can run the gamut from curiosity to violence to passion.

Was that why I felt so protective about Georgia's wine? Because in a dehumanized world natural wine is the symbol of all that is real and feeling? Natural wine can certainly be correct and flawless, but better still are those with the complexity of a flawed beauty. There can be a little volatility, a little breathlessness, an uncontrolled changeability. In a world where there is plenty of fake, the wines made naturally are honest.

This was John's point. Qvevri wine wasn't analogous to just any music, but especially with Georgia's polyphony and its many webbed imperfections that meld together. It is linked to the beauty of blended sound waves, which come together in harmony and disharmony. It is about the camaraderie of experiencing wine in the same way as someone else. It is about the harmony of connection, almost like a shared hallucination. Polyphony is multivoiced, but it smacks of history and culture, of music and religion. Its magic is woven into music, and that music holds the fabric of Georgian wine itself. John's point was complicated enough, mind-bending as well. But in the end, as Stefan's father played in the living room, it all became clearer to me.

"There is the connection to vibrancy and vibrations," John had said. The legless goatskin, as played by the elder man in the living room, was plaintive, and one skin bleated out a hypnotic web of sounds, polyphony out of one instrument. The sound seemed to reach right down to my big toe. Georgian wine, when done right, hits those vibrations. The lapsed shepherd was going to make wonderful wine.

We prepared to leave and were prevented by the call for one more toast from Stefan's father. I wasn't fearful; this was Adjara and not Guria; I didn't expect to be trapped this time. But I didn't expect the toast to concern me.

"To your brother's health," the father said. "May he thrive. Most important, next year, you bring him to us. We will help him heal."

I promised, even though I knew the promise was a feeble one. I so very much wanted to believe Georgia's sorcery could bring health. The only thing that Georgia could help me with at this point was its love.

Moved by the sound of the plaintive instrument, the prayers for my brother, and Stefan's wine, which I hoped I would get to taste, I imagined the day when I would meet his fans in Paris or London or Sydney or Verona, and Stefan would proudly show his wines and his country to the world. It would profoundly change his life, and the band of natural winemakers throughout Georgia, not just those in the east, would thrive and become known.

With a happy Camille in the backseat babbling about it all, Georgia had proved to be as exotic and yet as civilized a place as she'd ever been. We stopped along the way, by the side of the Black Sea at the road stands, to buy the grape-sized, intensely aromatic *pekhva*.

By the time we arrived at Iago's, John had received a call that the qvevri had arrived in the Loire, and Gela was busy burying them in Thierry Puzelat's winery. It was time for celebratory Chinuri. After all the years of shipping barrels out of the country, France was actually importing a different vessel. But first we toured Iago's new winery, which had double the amount of qvevri. "And where's Marina's qvevri?" I asked, eager to see the continuation of his wife Marina's wine.

Iago looked hangdog.

"But why!" I gasped. It seemed incomprehensible. The wine was so very good. It was so important for women to be seen in the wine world, as it can in truth get to be too much of a boys' club.

"There was no room; I needed all the qvevris this year," Iago explained.

"Marina and Téa didn't get their qvevri?" I repeated. I mean, how could he? The doting husband Iago? How could he not take care of his wife? I was crushed.

He looked crestfallen. Marina looked at her husband with love but as if she was about to give him a playful smack on the side of his head and say, "You see?"

"Next year," Iago promised us.

Georgia was sending me one lesson after another, including the one that what is truly yours can never be lost. If Marina and Téa's wines were truly theirs, they would come back. I tried to get past the disappointment. I was presented with a Sharpie and we all signed Iago's new wall, and then I commenced with my last feast.

....

AJARIAN CHIRBULI

Initially I thought that John was creating this breakfast dish from his head, but it turns out it's a version of an Ajarian *chirbuli*, the region's classic breakfast dish. It both tastes and looks very much like a relative to the Israeli *shakshuka*, where the eggs are poached in the sauce, the tomatoes, and the spice. Where it differs is the luscious use of fresh herbs.

Being a heat lover, John adds his own twist; it suits me and seems perfectly Georgian: he layers in some green hatch chilies. If you'd rather, you could add any hot pepper or a little hot *adjika*. It goes exceedingly well with *chacha*, by the way, though you might then want to go right back to sleep.

2 onions
2 tablespoons butter or oil
1 teaspoon cornmeal
2 juicy tomatoes
1 medium-sized hot chili, chopped (optional)
10 walnuts
1 clove garlic
½ cup fresh green coriander
½ cup dill
½ cup basil
4 eggs
½ teaspoon dried coriander
1 heaped teaspoon red pepper
salt to taste

Chop the onions and fry in butter on a low temperature for 4–5 minutes, stirring frequently.

Add 1 teaspoon cornmeal. Mix with the onions.

Chop the tomatoes and chili and add to the pan of fried onions.

Grind the walnuts. Crush the garlic, then cover the walnuts and garlic with water and bring to the boil. Reduce the temperature to low and add this walnut/garlic mixture to the tomato mixture. Add the ½ teaspoon of dried coriander, heaped teaspoon of red pepper, and salt. Stir thoroughly. Continue to cook on a low heat for 2–3 minutes.

Stir and continue to cook on a very low heat for 4 minutes, stirring frequently.

Chop the fresh green coriander, dill, and basil and add to the pan.

Stir thoroughly and reduce heat to very low. Either cook the eggs separately, poaching them carefully and then placing them in the sauce, or carefully crack the eggs and pour onto the *chirbuli* sauce.

Continue to cook for 2–3 minutes. The yolk of the eggs should be runny. Remove from heat and serve immediately.

CHAPTER 14

THE POWER OF BUTCHKI

It was 2014. An entire year had passed since I had last been in Georgia and stood inside the idle silkworm house. The worms had now gone to their final transformation, their silk safe and snug in cocoons and their speck-sized black eggs saved for the next season.

The rickety worm shack, a splintery thing from who knows when, had sunk a few inches more into the earth since I had last visited Lamara's little Eden behind the stone wall. Of course I wasn't alone. As always there were tagalongs. That was fine because to see others fall under Lamara's spell is a thing of beauty. I remembered what it was like to meet her for the first time. First times, first loves, first tastes — they and they alone can surprise the jaded. Of course, those with us were entranced listening to her impassioned story of the lifecycle of the silkworm.

It was easy to have a crush on Lamara. I certainly did. She's a fierce Kakhetian woman. She has warrior energy, tempered with femininity. Her passion for the ancient coupled with her admiration for the wisdom of historic medical remedies is seductive. Her obsession with raising silkworms is compelling. I could easily envision her wearing medieval robes, living in the cave city of Vardzia, playing a regal and important role, a figure in an epic poem. But what was it that makes me feel so connected to her, I wondered.

In Georgia, it's as if my emotions — always too raw and intense for my own good — seemed normal. Less timid, I was freer to be myself without guard — whether it was riffing on civilization and plumbing in a vineyard in Imereti, having soul connections with a bishop, or feeling entrapped in Guria. There was honesty and passion around me no matter which of the regions I went to or which people I communed with. I felt it with the people; I tasted it in the wine. With my first taste of Kisi, years before I ever dreamt of traveling there, my interest was piqued. And that was how I had felt when I had first met Lamara.

I hugged my weathered jean jacket around me and walked outside to where Lamara's new husband, Gocha, stood coaxing the flickering into flames. A work table lay low next to him.

Lamara was new to the married life. The two had known each other as children, but Gocha had gone on to marry another, and she never did. Once widowed, he pursued her, his schoolboy love. She put him off — to punish him for taking another path, she said. What she didn't say was why she allowed him to convince her to give up the solo life and become part of a couple. She, past fifty, had a hard time with the transition, something I could very much relate to. I watched him carefully to find out who this man was who had been able to convince Lamara to marry for the first time.

Gocha began his work. He skewered rectangular pieces of floppy yet firm cheeses, around which he then wrapped silky dough.

The others emerged from the hut; Lamara's piccolo voice trilled. John Wurdeman translated her musical Georgian. Lamara came over and grabbed the pierced cheese and dough and started to paint them slick with marigold-colored egg yolk. Gocha stuck them into the fire, transforming them into the artery-clogging delight. Satisfied, Lamara linked arms with me. We walked under the mulberry and walnut trees, up the stairs to the balcony where dinner was to be taken. The table was orderly at this point, adorned with the perennials: feathery greens, bushy stalks of tarragon, cut tomatoes, pickles, the salt cures — *jonjoli* this time instead of acacia flowers — various white salty cheeses, sautéed purslane, and the fish they call cat, whether it's cat fish or carp (but no matter what they called it, I couldn't ever bring myself to sample it, as it without fail looked so particularly dead).

In John's new entourage was a group of Frenchmen filming a documentary on France's love for Georgian qvevri wines and a lovely, slightly goofy writer from Toronto, happily wearing his gray felt Georgian fez-like skullcap. Whether it was in the desert or in a vineyard, he was always balancing his computer on one knee, as if doing the eagle yoga pose, taking notes. But that night he was with us, completely in the moment. There were also two young protégés of John's, both in their twenties. Both had started qvevri projects. Alex Rodzianko, from Tuxedo Park, had built a Signaghi winery; the other, Nathan Moss from England, was to make his first qvevri cider. During the year I had gone missing, John had birthed a little natural wine think tank around himself. Along with two other new wineries in the miniscule town, John had turned Signaghi into a one-stop destination for qvevri lovers.

I sat at the end of the table opposite from where Lamara and Gocha sat side by side, each taking turns going down to the kitchen to bring up more food to pile on the table, which started to appear dangerously laden. The polenta-like porridge and the eggplants and walnut sauce and the cheese breads could feed me for a year; the dumplings, *kinkhali*, pinched together like a pasha's plump turban, were then added to the meal, crowding the once orderly surface. I could barely glimpse the tablecloth below. I thought how rare it was for a rural woman who had never been out of the country, who hadn't traveled, to sit at the head of her own table with her husband. In this case I had the feeling that Lamara allowed her husband to share the role of toastmaster with her, rather than, as other people would see it, that her husband allowed *her* to sit there with him. An untraditional couple in a traditional home.

Chunky moths darted around our illuminated spirits. Lamara had let her hair down. She raised her glass in her hand. Her turquoise ring was prominent as she clutched the stem. She took control and drank us the toast: guests are sent from God.

She shoved her glass into the center of the table above the food and yelled, "*Butchki!*" We had a moment of hesitation and then we got the cue, sort of understanding that her call meant that we were to make a bush out of our glasses for a clink. We bunched our ourselves into one big traffic jam of a clink and chanted, "*Butchki, butchki, butchki!*" giggling out the words.

The talk tumbled. Very soon Lamara, in her generosity, started to channel more homeopathic remedies — not quite a party trick; she knew we loved them.

"The healthiest meat you can eat is sheep," she proclaimed. "For terminal illness, the best kind of sheep is raised on the very salty Borjomi water."

I remembered that Givi had told me that Stalin loved sheep from that very area in Meskheti that had salty grass. How was it that even Stalin knew the remedy? I asked, "How do you know this?"

"Everyone knows this," she said, "but the sources for me were medical books from the tenth through twelfth centuries. I've been reading and studying for years."

Next she wanted to tell us about eyes. "What do you do for an eye injury? Boil an egg. Then remove the yolk and put in a few drops of honey where the yolk was. Leave it overnight, and in the morning there will be a gel. One or two drops in your eye will help any injury."

We *butchkied*.

"And snails are also very good."

Lamara's husband nodded his head affirmatively and then added, "I put a snail on a wart; forty hours later the snail was gel and the wart was gone."

I flashed to an image of a snail strapped to his finger as he wagged his wart-free index at us.

"*Butchki, butchki, butchki!*"

We were drinking seriously. I was experiencing joy from wine, flushed and with a heightened connection, though I was not drunk. It was hard for me to actually get drunk, as if there was always an internal switch that shut off. Even in Georgia I couldn't get that control button to turn off, or perhaps I merely embodied the Georgian saying (one that was often rebelled against by others), "Never get drunker than your guests." And the other saying, "Wine is healthy, as long as you keep focus." So I might have not been drunk, but let's go with tipsy.

I kept my focus. I felt guilty, looking over at our heroic designated driver and future cider maker, Nathan, drinking water instead of the Mtsvane in our glasses. But when next was I going to be in Georgia in this very way and moment, in the open, with the stars and planets pulsing above us? Never. I needed to live it; I needed to drink and eat in unchecked caution. The wine was singing in all its amber grittiness, and John refilled my glass for me. I thought, So what if I drink past my cutoff point?

I wanted to tell Lamara she could go off duty; she knew I loved the wise medicine lessons, but it was time for her to just be with us. As if she heard me, she picked up her wine. We were silenced. A toast was coming, one that I had hoped she was going to forget. But it was tradition, and even if she delayed it, mercifully, it had to happen.

"Family members," she said solemnly, "who pass away are still connected to us."

There it was.

It was the requisite toast—remembering those who were no longer with us—even if it came a little later in the evening than tradition demanded.

When I left Georgia in the wet harvest of 2013, my brother had already left the experimental treatment program, as he said, "to go home to die with dignity." Two days after I arrived home from Georgia, my mother and I boarded a plane to see him, to say our good-byes to him as he lay under the veil of morphine. One week later we pitched dirt onto his coffin in the relentless rain. When in public, I couldn't be sure when the grief would come. Sitting at the table, I didn't want to feel the cramping under my cheekbone as I fought for control of my emotions. Alone with Lamara I could let go. Sure. But not in front of this international table, including people I barely knew. The tears stayed in place.

"They worry about us," Lamara continued. "They are happy when we are well. We will one day be in that world with them." Then looking at me, she said, "May he rest in eternal peace."

I hadn't told her, but she knew. Of course she knew. The tears escaped. As long as I didn't have to talk, they could just fall gently, quietly, with no one taking too much notice. I took in a breath to try to relax and unwrinkle the tension bunching in my face.

When John had first brought me to see Lamara, he thought he was just bringing me to meet someone important in his life. Working on intuition, he wanted to make sure I got to experience a remaining piece of Georgian culture: the last silk spinner standing and one of the keepers of homeopathic wisdom. But once behind those walls I found he had guided me there for something else—a parallel to Georgian wine. A death and a resurrection, a continual life cycle, important where the past is not forgotten.

"When my own brother died," Lamara said, looking directly at me, "the silkworms were what kept me alive."

I hadn't known about her brother's death.

"When did he die?" I asked her.

It turns out that it wasn't long before my own brother was diagnosed, just before I had met her. That was why, I realized in looking back, that as she was showing me how she spun the silk between her fingers with her perfectly painted nails, she stopped abruptly when John told her my brother was sick. Some don't feel that brother connection, but I have since met some who know immediately what this particular love was, as if it made us eligible for some sort of secret society. Lamara belonged to that society and had looked at me with those pecan-shell-colored eyes, full of fearful concern, and asked, "What kind of cancer? What stage?"

By the time I got there on that Yom Kippur season, I already believed in the supernaturalness of Georgia. But that year I needed to believe in magic. And it was as if Georgia, its wine, and Lamara could offer it to me. Unexplained connections and intuitions—she and I shared those. We also shared the connection, love, and loss of a much-loved and much-felt sibling.

"The worms can feel me when I come into the silk house," Lamara said. "They get this . . . excitement when they feel me. I learn so much from them, from their cycles, from their transformation and resurrection. When my brother died, a piece of me was cut off, and it was easier to keep the door closed. Working with the silkworms taught me about the rhythm of transformation. It helped me come to life again."

I did not have the silkworms to teach me any lessons. I would have to learn secondhand, from her and from Georgia.

And as we had done every time someone said something warm and profound, we brought our glasses together and cried, "*Butchki, butchki, butchki!*"

But Lamara wasn't finished. "I would like to live a life like my grandmother. Up until she was ninety-six she was filled with tales and stories. She lived a colorful and rich life. A person who can die with laughter—that's a good life. May we live a life full of color. May we be able to live in such a way. May we go down in such a path."

Andrew had a wife he loved and children he loved, but he died without ever telling me what had made him stop laughing freely. But if he didn't die with laughter, his seriously wry irony never left him. But the irony did not stop him from telling me for the first and last time that he loved me.

Lamara continued: "When we meet God in the afterworld, may we say thank you for giving us such a wonderful life. May we leave the world in such a way that we leave much for the next generations."

We started to move our glasses toward each other for a solemn meeting.

"If you don't look in the eyes of your fellow drinkers when you're toasting, its seven years of bad sex," John added, and this wasn't Georgian but merely international wine-toasting etiquette. We all *butchkied*.

Comic relief was welcome. But the bond had been stitched together at the table. John has said that one can feel closer to someone that one sits next to at a *supra* than to a neighbor one has known for twenty years because the nature of talk at a *supra* cuts through the superficialities. I thought that was just John talking, as he tends to be that way—emotional and immediate. But it is the structure of the *supra*, and the flowing of wine that supported it, that prompts intimacy.

There was a plan to go hiking in the Garedgi desert the next day, so an early wake-up call was in order. It was well after one in the morning; I didn't want to leave. Our Canadian gentleman didn't want to leave either. He brought out some Cuban cigars to the delight of Gocha. Even Lamara lit up. What would another hour hurt? Gocha tried to get us to stay. The wine was poured anew. The newly married man stood up and started to speak.

"Everything is rooted in wine," Gocha said with authority. "Even spirituality, love, and relationships are compared to wine."

Yes, he was a good match for Lamara, I thought. Even though Gocha had traveled, had had a career in business, his toast showed me that wine touched everyone in this country, even if a person didn't make it.

"Before you take wine into you," Gocha said, "before you put wine on its feet, caressing it is necessary. Something so sacred, divine, and godly should become the core of your being. Making and drinking wine is a process of gratitude. When a person is full of love, that love becomes more intense because of wine. The drink is not merely an alcoholic beverage. It is the means for deep communication with other people. And in this way, life and wine need caressing."

It was a profound tone poem to wine, I thought. The point of difference about wine's place in Georgia compared to any other place in the world is that it was drunk as well as contemplated. It is connected with culture, with love, with gratitude. It is still so among the small winemakers and hopefully will never be merely a commercial endeavor. There may come a time when there are Georgian "winemakers," instead of wine shepherds, but for now they are serving the past by bringing it to the present. No matter what comes in the future, they will never forget it. After all, there will be a time in a *supra* when we toast to who and what are no longer with us. Wine has a seasonality the way the worm does; it has life, death, and resurrected life again.

We absorbed the message and sat with it as the crickets chirped. Everywhere there were parables. Georgia's love affair with the vine has been going on for eight thousand years, give or take a few. I, for one, didn't care who was the first to bring wine to the world or who had been the first qvevri master who learned how to fashion clay ropes into fermentation vessels. The first kinds of wines had to be those made with skin contact. I was sure. The vessel in which they were made, the qvevri, was the ultimate tool in nurturing a sane and healthy wine into the glass.

What I had come to learn during my travels — six visits in and hopefully many more to come — was that there is no other place on earth so plaited with wine, where that vibrant transformative drink is considered so noble, so spiritual that a country would die for its right to grow it and make it the way it wants to — naturally, with no additives, even with some irregularities, as long as it gives pleasure.

Consultants will come — oh they will! They'll come to tell the winemaking Georgians how to work and what to do. There will be consultants to encourage Chardonnay instead of Chinuri. There will be marketers who will push for a consistent wine to be delivered to the public. There will be the Californian (Mr. Reverse Osmosis) and his ilk insisting, "Buy my technology, my powders, my potions, and my machines." People will come to destroy these emotional wines in the name of civilization. People will try to turn Georgian wine into something boring and conventional. But they don't know Georgia. Some may buckle, but this is a country where a winemaker, Ilia Chavchavadze, was also the leading intellectual light of modern Georgia and a saint. This is a country where a bishop has revived wine and where an old man will stand up and shout, "Are you telling me God did not give the grape everything it needs to make wine naturally?" This is a country where a poem about unconditional love is at its core.

There is a new group of winemakers who are working with the vessel and the grape and their ancient tools. They are the sum of their past and will fight for their wine because they know the truth — as Gocha and Lamara and John and Niki and Ramaz and Iago and Marina and Gogi and Didimi and Soliko and Gela know, as will all of the new ones coming on board and all I've yet to meet — that what we're talking about is a drink that is far more than just fermented grapes.

As the cigar came my way and I quickly declined, I raised my glass. Then we all raised our glasses. Lamara cried, "*Butchki!*" And we made a bush of clinks and toasts as Jupiter glowed above us.

LAMARA'S FERMENTED ACACIA FLOWERS

Whereas I always have a bowl of olives on the table, in Georgia one of the first dishes on the table is *jonjoli. Jonjoli*, a salt-fermented delicacy, is typically made from the blooms of the bladderwort bush. Lamara often improvises with acacia flowers. The result is a little more delicate and fabulously habit forming.

Collect the flowers when they are still buds, before the bugs get into them (this happens quickly, so collect them as soon as the buds appear). At this point the flowers have the best healing properties. Wash them quickly. Choose a pickling jar and layer the flowers with fennel stalks and salt. Press very tightly; use branches from the fennel stalk. Leave there until they ferment, about 2 weeks. As Lamara says, *jonjoli* can stay there throughout the winter.

POSTSCRIPT

And so what happened to that man I fought with at the beginning of this journey, the one I met when Niki took me to that party at Culinarium? That argumentative, chain-pulling man who unwittingly sent me on a journey one jet-lagged night when he poured me a terribly inferior rosé from France and told me that organic wine was bullshit. Had he changed too?

It was on my mind to find out. But I wasn't sure I was up for it.

"Come to Culinarium with us tonight," John said.

I balked. "I'm not sure I want to go," I answered.

"But why?" he asked.

"It's my last night, and I want a comfort zone," I said. But of course I wanted to hang with him and the others during my last hours in Georgia, even if it wasn't exactly what I wanted to do. It was poetic that I should circle back to the starting point of a journey, so I started to reconsider. "What's going on?"

"Jeremy is going to preside over a Chinese menu and Chinuri tasting," he answered.

"What?" I asked. Jeremy was the sommelier from Chicago who had come to change his life in Georgia, the very same guy who had jumped into Iago's qvevri to help him scrub them.

"You don't know that "Chinuri" is the Georgian word for 'Chinese'?"

"No," I said. I then knew ten words in Georgian instead of nine.

"We'll pair Chinuri with the Chinese appetizers that Tekuna will prepare. It's stupid. It might not work, but it will be fun, and everyone will be there so you'll get to see them all."

"Will that man, the one I fought with, be there?"

"Who cares?" John didn't really grasp that I was shy about returning to the scene of that incident.

I cared, but I gave in. "Okay. It's totally cool. I can deal with him."

If there were more arguments, I'd be there with my people and armed with a depth of knowledge about Georgia and why the organic and natural mattered. I was ready.

It was winter in Georgia. In the roadside stalls, hooked pigs' heads, river fish, and planks of squash marked our route to visit a winemaker near the Armenian border.

Driving south, I thought about how quickly things can move in that wonderful country. It had been only four months since my last steps on Georgian ground, and the moment seemed perfect. Putin was almost behaving. The plumbing and electricity were more efficient. There were almost too many new wine producers to keep track. There were sparks of life in the lost regions. More women were jumping into the qvevris. John's town of Signaghi had been reborn as a tourist-ready natural wine destination. The World Bank had stepped up and pitched in to develop Bishop Davit's plan for Qvevri House at Ikalto. The small growers were no longer *boganos*, no longer farmers without land. They were purchasing land and farming it. The dream to be a wine shepherd was being realized. And as far as cross-pollination, there was an increasing stream of Americans and Danes coming to Georgia for that . . . fairy dust, as evidenced by Jeremy.

The weather was warmer near the border. The land seemed unassuming, less dramatic. The winemaker's Mtsvane was solid, and we feasted, knowing that there was a long night ahead of us, especially for me, as I would not have time between the sheets before my 6:00 a.m. flight. As we left, the *chacha* materialized. I smelled mine, and it was pretty mousey, so I snuck off unseen and pitched it into a plant. But the poor sommelier, Jeremy, was cornered into doing shots. The winemaker had been a pretty serious military man at one time, and there was no saying no to him. The sommelier promptly fell asleep in the backseat as we drove back to Tbilisi. We had about an hour to recoup, regroup, and head to the evening.

I walked over and saw the lemony lights of the Culinarium window silhouetting the little square in Vera. The school was inviting and filled with the kinds of modern Georgians with whom I hadn't come in contact much, but around the big communal table were the core group of chummy winemakers with whom I'd spent so much time. Seeing Niki with an empty chair beside him at the table, I took it.

I looked up at the blackboard that showed the wines by the glass. I did a clear double take; I wasn't sure if I had read the board correctly. There in English it said, "Our selection of organic wines."

"Something has changed, indeed!" I said. "Is that guy here? You know, the one I fought with the night you took me here?"

Understanding me, Niki smiled and softly said, "You are safe, Alice. He is no longer a partner."

I suppose as I saw in front of me a transformation from "Bio is bullshit" to "Our organic wines," he had to have been gone. I felt a wild sense of relief, as if the troops had receded. With rooting eyes I scanned the room like a detective and saw, as if a vine running away from the Turks (or at least the natural wine police), one conventional bottle hiding out.

We were late to start, and our wineglasses were empty. "Where is Jeremy?" I asked John.

"Don't know," he said looking concerned. He called him again and said to me, "It keeps on going to voice mail."

"This is really strange," I said to John. "I mean, he's a professional. You just do not *not* show up. Is he even alive?"

"Don't get hysterical," John said to me. Then shrugging to Tekuna, he gave in to having to run the show.

"Friends," he boomed out, switching between Georgian and English. Then we were off with a brand new Chinuri from Stalin's home town, Ateni.

As the event progressed, I noticed that a few of the guests were

confounded over the cloudy Pheasant's Tears in their glasses and arguing if it was correct or not. "Is it supposed to look like that?" they
asked John.

John walked over with the bottle, plunked his thumb over the opening, dramatically shook it up, and poured it anew. Now the wine had
progressed from cloudy to pure fog. "Try it now," he said.

They marveled. The wine was different. Almost more complete.

"That is the magic of natural wine," John said, ever evangelical.

At the end of the evening Tekuna came to sit next to me. She was
working her own battle against the staunch traditions of Georgian
cuisine, frustrated with a lack of creativity and a focus merely on the
past. It was difficult to bring a more sophisticated form of cuisine to
a city where rustic restaurants, which looked like home kitchens, were
more the norm. I complimented her on a quince soup and a beetroot
cake—take a carrot cake and just substitute beets—and I asked her
about the missing partner. She was one of the few people who hadn't
known about my fight with him, but she listened with amusement.
"He didn't belong here," she said.

"And what do you think about naturally made qvevri wine?" I
asked her.

She's a woman who had traveled for work throughout the world—
Singapore, New York, London. She took a sip of Iago's Chinuri and
said, "If you care about your ingredients, it's the only way."

If only the rest of the world—the big chefs, the small chefs, those
who believe in seasonal and organic—would realize that wine is also
food. Was it so damned difficult to understand?

Time to get rowdy. We walked over to Ghvino Underground, and
on the way I examined the wonderful parade of past and future. The
women winemakers of Georgia were out! Marina and Téa were no
longer the only contenders. They had been joined by a twenty-five-
year-old dance lover named Mariam Iosebidze, who had just made
her first vintage of Dancing Girl wine. Other changes? Iago had just
finished his first year of the dream: he was now a full-time winemaker.

Perhaps there will be the fancy boys and girls going to Tbilisi's wine school, looking for the cushy life technology can give, but never mind; the natural wine movement in Georgia was safely on its way. At about midnight the crowd burst into applause as Jeremy, looking a little ragged and sheepish, descended the steps into the wine bar.

He had been done in by the *chacha*.

The bottles flowed. There must have been at least thirty of us drinking and talking in a way that seemed impossible back in the States. Ideas and friendship and wine — these are what mattered, even as the world was going to hell elsewhere. We drank more wine.

There were only a few hours to go before my flight back home, and going to bed was irrelevant. But when it came time to prepare for the short trip to the airport, John, who had started his Georgian romance two decades ago, walked me back along the darkened river. We stood for what seemed like a long time on the bridge over the water, in the city in the country where I had come to look for magic, or at least answers.

"So John, did Stefan ever get vines in Ajara?" I asked.

"The shepherd? Yes. He now has half a hectare of Chkhaveri planted in his mountain village of Qvashta, courtesy of Gela and John. It's a start."

"And any other news that I need to know about?"

It turned out that Thierry, Gela, and John had bought some vineyard land near the Pompeii of wine. Death and life restored. Wine and its meaning in a senseless world. I suppose Georgia will always be connected to issues that are large and powerful for me. To my brother. To friendship. To wine and to love. I would have wanted to have been part of that rebirth in Meskheti. Yet even if I couldn't plant the vines in a land where they were almost forgotten, I will one day drink that wine from a glass, a *piala* or a *kantsi*, as friends revive what could have been lost, what was the past, and what will be the future.

The city was glistening, twinkling, impossibly romantic, crumbling with the past and embracing graceful new architecture, like the bridge in front of me that crawled over the river like a snail. The paradox didn't jar me. I embraced it.

TEKUNA'S ELARJI BALLS WITH ALMOND BAJE

With travel come new ideas. People will travel to Georgia to get the idea of how to return to simplicity, and Georgians will pick up new flavors and techniques by traveling. It's inevitable. The trick for growth or fusion is to always have the flavor of the past somewhere hidden. In that way Tekuna is the future. The positive future. She is steeped in traditional cooking and taking it to a star cuisine stage.

Elarji is from a region of Georgia I hadn't gone to, Samegrelo. It's a twist on the popular polenta cakes, *mchadi*.

> 2 cups cornmeal or grits
> 8 cups water
> ½ pound smoked sulguni (or a combination of smoked
>   gouda or mozzarella), grated
> ¾ cup flour
> eggs
> ⅓ cup panko bread crumbs

Cook the cornmeal or grits slowly in the water on a low temperature. When it's done, add the grated cheese and stir it in one direction until the cheese melts completely. Put the hot mixture on a shallow dish, wait for it to cool, and then shape it into ping pong–sized balls. Roll them in the flour, then dip them in eggs and panko. Keep cool in the refrigerator until ready to begin serving. Fry them for 5-7 minutes. Serve with almond *baje*.

ALMOND BAJE

1¾ cups skinned almonds
1 teaspoon red curry paste
1 teaspoon Svaneti salt (see chapter 3)
½ teaspoon dry coriander
½ teaspoon marigold flower
chili powder to taste
salt and pepper to taste
water

Put all the ingredients in a blender and blend well. Add water slowly until a smooth sauce forms. Season with salt and pepper if needed.

Keep it in the refrigerator until ready for use.

ACKNOWLEDGMENTS

How does an artist convince a government agency to commission a series of essays that are not didactic and not obviously promotional? I have no idea, but that's what John Wurdeman did. Five months after he had that big fat idea, I was sitting with the then chairman of Georgia's National Wine Agency, Levan Davitashvili, on a bench outside of Ghvino Underground. I think we were drinking Didimi's Krakhuna, and he told me how much he believed in the natural wine-makers. He then said, "Now, let's do that chapbook." That chapbook was called *Skin Contact*. The end result, *For the Love of Wine*, would have been impossible without the inspiration, assistance, encouragement, translations, laughter, craziness, drinking, and friendship of John. It wouldn't have been possible without a government agency that sets a world standard for commitment to real wine. And so those men and the forward thinking National Wine Agency, now lead by Giorgi Samanishvili, head the long list of *madlobas*.

But before I could even begin to write, there were the wines. Wine importer and all-round incredible man Chris Terrell provided me with my first tastes and then conspired to haul me over to that first qvevri symposium. After I started to write, there was a whole other classification of assistance. As far as the physical sculpting and snipping goes, the input of Sue Shapiro (and our Thursday night group) was invaluable. As a result they know more about Georgian wine—and natural wine—than they ever cared to know. Melissa Clark, as always, was a constant cheerleader and provider of sage advice. A dyslexic, I am reliant on selfless editors. My cousin Ann Kugel helped edit the original manuscript as did Doreen Schmid. Liz Reisberg is always on call to edit. Another favorite editor is my mother, Ethel. She is a force. All helped me to get this on the desk of my editor at Nebraska, Kristen Elias Rowley. Kristen responded immediately to the material and gave it a fine home. Since the first email contact she was a total delight to deal with. Later on in the process her editorial assistant, Emily Wendell, and, my project editor, Joeth Zucco, proved to be an enormous help. Still later I was lucky enough to work with Bojana Ristich, who blessed me with her careful copyediting.

Recipe collection was a group effort. Wonderful cooks fueled the possibilities, starting with the initial cooking of the Mothers of Shuamta Convent at the Alaverdi Monastery and continuing to the many feasts with many winemaking families. Luarsab Togenidze and Nino Mamulaishvili always had the doors of their restaurant, Azarphesha, open to me. John Wurdeman and Ketevan Mindorashvili tweaked my selections for authenticity. Cider maker Nathan Moss was my conduit to the uber-talented chef of the Pheasant's Tears wine bar, Gia Rokashvili, and his wife, Tamro Janiashvili Rokashvili, both of whom provided me with recipe missing links and plenty of culinary inspiration.

Ketevan (or Keto) lent me her husband over and over again. Not only that, but she also gave me her friendship and her music and educated me on me how *chacha* could be the direct path to spirituality. She also shared her violet *chacha*, which to this violet lover was thrilling.

Tina Kezeli at the Georgian Wine Agency gave me my very own copy of Otar Iosseliani's *Falling Leaves*, which I watched on repetitive loop, continually finding inspiration within. Irakli Cholobargia at the National Wine Agency fielded my questions and put up with my nagging for maps. Giorgi Barishivilli allowed the use of his wonderful photos. Ia Tabagari of Living Roots procured me books, travel arrangements, bookings, and schedules, including those with Bondo Kalandadze, master booze man, who shared his historic knowledge of wine and spirit making during the Soviet era; wine ethnologist Levan Pruidze, who gave me the academic side; and Givi Chagelishvili, who regaled me with Stalin-inspired wine stories.

I want to thank all of the brave winemakers who helped me, ferried me, and housed me during The Great Alice Handoff: John Wurdeman, Gela Patashvili, Metropolitan Bishop Davit of Alaverdi, Father Gerasime, Niki Antadze, Iago Bitarishvili and Marina Kurtanidze, Kakha Berishvili, Alexi Tsikhekishvili, Nika Bakhia, Malkhaz Jackelli, Soliko Tsaishvili and Nino Mikelaishvili, Ramaz Nikoladze and Nestan, and Lamara Bezhashvili. A special shout-out to the medievals: Queen Tamar and Shota Rustaveli, who still nurture the country by keeping the women strong, the men poets, and the wines honest. Finally, a thank-you to every single one of the winemakers who opened up their *maranis* (wineries) and qvevris and who shared their stories and their time. All have had a part in this journey, which will never feel finished.

9 781612 347646